KU-258-191

CHINESE CHILDHOOD

In 1973 Pollock's Toy Museum in London organised a small exhibition of 'Chinese Childhood'. As we set to work to prepare the catalogue, we realised that not only were we indebted to China for the invention of gunpowder, silk, paper, porcelain, the wheelbarrow, the magnetic navigational compass and other technical discoveries listed in the history books, but for many other more delightful things also: for roses and pandas; for tops and diabolos; for spillikins, puppets, puzzles, kites . . . . . .
This picture book is the result of our researches into the world of Chinese childhood—a world which is in some ways strangely close to that of children in many other parts of the globe.

The Scroll of A Hundred Sons: riding hobby horses.

CHINESE CHILDHOOD

Marguerite Fawdry

Pollocks Toy Theatres Limited

To my Grandson Edmond Lincoln Fawdry

CENTRAL LIBRARY
WITHDRAWN
BRITISH MUSEUM

13126

BRITISH MUSEUM
23 DEC 1980
WITHDRAWN
EDUCATION SERVICE

First published in the USA by
Barron's,
113 Crossways Park Drive,
Woodbury, New York 11797.

First published in the UK by
Pollock's Toy Theatres Limited
1 Scala Street, London W1.

© Marguerite Fawdry 1977.

Produced by
Blaketon Hall Limited, London for
Pollock's Toy Theatres Limited and
Barron's, New York.

Designed by Melvyn Gill Design Associates Ltd.

All Rights Reserved.

ISBN 0 9505588 0X

Printed in Great Britain by
Hazell Watson & Viney Ltd,
Aylesbury, Bucks

CONTENTS

Overture:
THE SCROLL OF
A HUNDRED SONS

In the Department of Oriental Antiquities of the British Museum there is a delicately painted hand scroll—an 18th century copy of an earlier Ming painting—entitled 'A Hundred Sons'. Six scenes from this scroll, depicting little boys riding hobby-horses, playing with puppets, feeding a phoenix, saying their prayers, beating drums and dancing have been reproduced as postcards. Let us look at the whole scroll and see what else these little 16th century Chinese boys are doing.

The scroll is called 'A Hundred Sons', but all the pictures are concerned with the activities of the same group of seven or eight

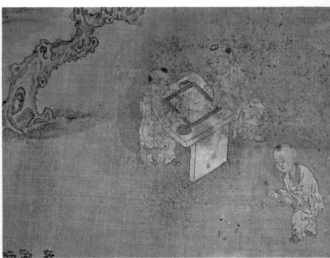

boys and their baby brother. In only one episode are they being naughty: two of the bigger boys are locked in a nasty hair-pulling fight. Otherwise all is serene in the elegant gardens and terraces where they are playing so decorously. This decorum, the presence of legendary animals, and the fact that the boys seem at one point to be playing at 'Hermits' or enacting a religious procession, all indicate some underlying didactic and moral purpose.

It is not difficult for us to conjure up the image of a Victorian paterfamilias gravely opening the family Bible, writing on its flyleaf the name of the latest addition to the family, reading a chapter, and then picking up for the benefit of the little ones gathered round him one of those edifying picture-books of moral stories.

This Chinese scroll fulfilled perhaps just such a purpose. One can imagine a well-to-do Chinese grandpapa, seated at a long, low table, his grandsons dutifully ranged round him, unrolling the scroll on which all the names of the revered ancestors were inscribed, and adding with deft, elegant strokes of his paintbrush the name of his lastborn grandson; then, for the entertainment of his brothers, unfurling the scroll of 'A Hundred Sons' and pausing, now and then, to add an explanation or a comment.

Three hundred years later, we in turn look at each little episode, adding as we do so more comments—and other pictures.

"A Hundred Sons".

CHAPTER ONE

PLAYING IN THE GARDEN

*In which the Scroll of a Hundred
Sons is unfurled, revealing children
dancing, tumbling, and playing drum and
cymbal; and in which they confront the Dragon
and the Phoenix and ride upon the Ch'i-Lin,
that fabulous creature of majestic gait
celebrated by the poet of the Imperial
Court five hundred years ago.*

Opposite: The Scroll: riding the Ch'i Lin.

In the first scene the baby is trying to stand on its head or turn a somersault; an elder boy is giving a piggy-back ride to a younger one; and the little boy in a red gown is dancing a jig, holding in one hand a long staff, while the others are making a merry din with drums, flute and clapper.

It would seem that they are playing at being acrobats—recreating for themselves the performance of some wandering troupe that had been called in to entertain the family on the occasion of a birthday or some other festivity. Indeed, their actions are not only mirrored in these modern paper-cuts and in the set of postage stamps issued in 1974, but foreshadowed in the postures of the acrobats we can observe on murals dating from the Han Dynasty 200 years BC—they too doing handstands and sword dances to the accompaniment of drums.

The next section takes us out of reality, into the world of the children's imagination. A sheet has been draped over the spear or staff the little boy was holding in his hand while dancing; the bigger boy is riding a strangely-coloured animal; and three others have climbed up on to a rock and with magic gestures have conjured up in the sky a fierce dragon. The little ones cower down in a rather scared huddle, while the brave boy in blue cautiously holds out a curly bit of fairy fungus to a huge, pheasant-like bird.

Below: The Scroll: piggy-back and dance.

*Above: A Hundred Sons
again — a favourite Chinese
decorative theme.*

The Ch'i-Lin

The Dragon and the Phoenix are as familiar to Chinese children as gryphons, Loch Ness monsters and runcible cats are to us. We too have met legendary Dragons and Phoenixes; but the Ch'i-Lin, like the Snow Lion and the Yeti, is an animal peculiar to China. It is said to have the body of a deer, the tail of an ox, horse's hooves, a variegated, tawny hide, and a single horn; but it is not part of the Greco-European species 'Pegasus Unicornis', nor is it a 'Centaurus Pennatus'.

We do now in fact know a great deal about the Ch'i-Lin, for it was seen in September 1415 by a great concourse of people gathered together at the Perfumed Gate of the Imperial Palace in the reign of the third Ming Emperor.

The Ch'i-Lin was for the Chinese a creature of good omen. It was the emblem of honest soldiers and upright judges. It was known to spare the innocent but to use its horn to pierce the guilty. The Ch'i-Lin could only become visible to men when a just

Cameleopard, from The History of Four Footed Beasts. Edward Topsel, 1607.

and good prince ruled the kingdom, when law and order reigned, and when the powers of Heaven were in perfect equilibrium.

Now it happened that in 1415 the Chinese fleet, under the command of its brilliant navigator Cheng-Ho (a Muslim eunuch from the province of Yunnan) returned to the China Seas from a long voyage to the Persian Gulf, bringing back many rare, exotic curiosities and strange animals to add to the imperial collection. Among them was a Ch'i-Lin.

After extolling the glory of the Emperor Yung-Le, a paragon among princes, the poet Shen Tu of the Academy of Letters gives us this description:

Opposite: Another Chinese version of the Ch'i Lin: a 20th century folk print.

> *A Ch'i-Lin has appeared amongst us,*
>
> *Standing fifteen feet tall,*
>
> *With horn of flesh, tail of ox, body of deer;*
>
> *Bright spots dapple its coat of gold;*
>
> *Its voice is that of a soft, melodious bell;*
>
> *In stately rhythm it moves, with graceful steps,*
>
> *Its hooved feet ever careful*
>
> *To preserve from harm all living creatures.*

Below: Modern paper-cuts from Shanghai: more realistic giraffes.

Shen Tu's Ch'i-Lin, this tall, gentle animal from the African grasslands, was called with equal astonishment by our Western forefathers a 'cameleopard'.

A Chinese Androcles

One winter's day long ago a poor woodcutter was chopping wood high up in the mountains when he heard a low whimpering coming from a nearby thicket.

The year before, the woodcutter had cut down a lot of bamboo stems, and round the roots sharp spears of wood had been left sticking out of the earth. As he walked through the grove, picking his way carefully, he suddenly saw before him a huge tigress. She was lying in a pool of blood: a tall shaft of bamboo had pierced her hind leg and pinned her to the ground. She looked up at the woodcutter and moaned gently.

"Poor beast," he said, "poor beast. I will go and get some help," and he quickly made his way down the mountain.

"Mother, mother," he called as he reached his home. "You must come and help me rescue a poor wounded animal. Bring some wine and water to bathe its leg."

Together mother and son climbed back up the mountain path, and while the son prepared to lift the tigress's leg off the cruel spike, the old mother sat down by its side and, patting its head, talked to it gently.

"There, there," she said, "the pain will soon be eased when my son has bathed and washed your wound; then it will heal up nicely. We are humble, poor people, so poor that my fine young son can't afford to get himself a wife. But we do our best, we do our best, working hard, doing no one any harm. Now, now, poor beast, I hope you'll soon be well, and perhaps some day you'll bring me a pretty young daughter-in-law. Well, now your leg is free we must be going. Good-bye, good-bye!" And bowing politely, the old woman and her son prudently hastened homewards.

Now it happened that some time after that a rich farmer, who lived a long way off on the other side of the mountain, had undertaken to marry his daughter off to one of his friends in a neighbouring town. The bridal procession set off in great pomp up the mountain tracks; but as the ascent grew steeper it came on to rain, and then to snow. The musicians stopped playing, and everyone wrapped themselves in their raincloaks.

Suddenly, at the top of the pass, five huge tigers appeared. The wedding party scattered in panic-stricken confusion: only the girl remained, trapped in her sedan chair.

At dawn the woodcutter opened his door. There, trembling from head to foot, stood a young girl, wrapped in a red bridal veil. Needless to say, mother and son welcomed her in with open arms.

The young man and the girl were soon married, and all three settled down happily together.

But not for long. The rich farmer sent out search parties and found out what had happened to his daughter. The woodcutter was arrested and accused of kidnapping the young girl. In vain his mother pleaded with the magistrate saying "We are not to blame. The tigers brought her to my door. My son is innocent. If you do not believe me, I will call the tigers to witness."

At that moment five tigers sprang roaring into the courtroom. Everyone fled except the judge. White and shaking, he nevertheless rose to his feet, saying "Did you?" The tigers bowed their heads, then raised them, their eyes flashing and their teeth bared.

"I believe you," said the judge hastily. "I declare the prisoner innocent. He is free to leave this court and return immediately with his bride to his mountain home."

Far right: One Hundred Children at play. Ink and colour on silk: Southern Sung Dynasty. (J.H.Wade Fund, Cleveland Museum of Art).

Right: Modern schoolgirl; traditional dance posture.

Below: Postage stamps, 1974: Chinese acrobats.

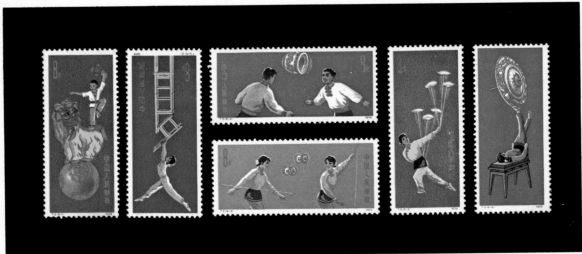

Tug-of-war.   *Gymnastics.*

CHAPTER TWO

DRAGONS

*Of Chinese Dragons: their nature,
habitat, transformations, and other
strange properties; of Dragon battles;
and of the origin of the Lakes known as the
Dragon's Tears. Of the Spring awakening of the
Dragons by Fireworks; of the Chinese
predilection for these explosives, and the
vexed matter of the invention of
gunpowder.*

According to an ancient Chinese writer a dragon has the head of a camel, the horns of a stag, the eyes of a demon, the ears of a cow, the neck of a snake, the scales of a carp and the claws of an eagle. On its head is a lump, which enables it to soar through the air. The male dragon has whiskers and an undulating horn: the female's nose is straight. There are yellow dragons, blue dragons, red, white and black dragons.

New-born Chinese dragons are tiny, like baby lizards, but they grow at a tremendous rate. They can also change their appearance, taking on at will the shape of a lovely girl, an old woman, a fish. The ancestors of the first emperors of China were reputed to have been dragons.

Some dragons breathe a special kind of fire, which flares up when it meets water. Their skins, even when cast off, shine in the night like pearls, coral and other precious stones. Their fossil bones when ground will cure a variety of illnesses, as will the

The Scroll: playing at dragons.

medicinal plants which spring up everywhere around the pools
where they take their winter sleep.

Winter in China is the season of drought. In the spring the
dragons wake up and begin to fight: thunderstorms break out and
rain pours down in torrents. If the dragon battles are too fierce,
fireballs fall to the ground and rivers rise in flood. To prevent
this, Chinese emperors would row along the river in beautiful
dragon-shaped boats, coaxing the dragons to be more mindful of
human needs.

In Chinese folk-tales dragons do not have quite the same nasty
habits as their Western cousins. They are not interested in captive
maidens, do not indulge in mortal combats with young men
armed to the teeth; nor do they live, breathing fire and
destruction, in wild, desolate heaths and mountains. Oriental
dragons live in crystal and coral palaces; their dragon emperors
have beautiful daughters whose idea of bliss is to leave the

Folded paper dragons.

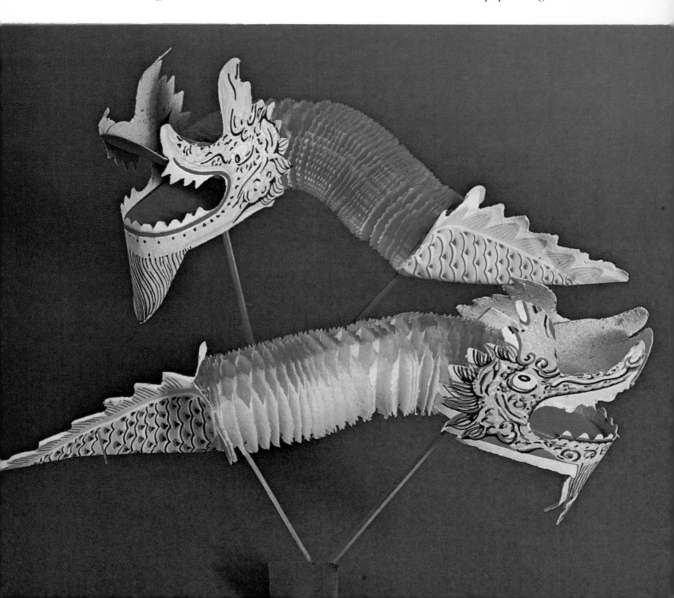

iridescent, watery splendour in which they have been brought up, and to settle down peacefully on land with some brave young peasant boy whose only wealth is a generous heart and simple, industrious habits.

Dragon's Tears

Above: Paper dragon.

Just such a boy features in the legend which tells how twenty-four small lakes in the province of Swechwan came to be called the Dragon's Tears. This boy's name was Wen P'eng. He lived with his widowed mother in a tiny cottage on the banks of the River Min. He was too young to work in the fields, so he spent his days fishing. His mother sold his catch in the nearby village, and so they managed to eke out a meagre living.

One evening at dusk Wen P'eng, who had caught nothing all day, cast his line desperately into the water. Suddenly he felt a great tug on his rod, and after a struggle he landed a huge, shining, golden fish.

"Wen P'eng," gasped the fish, "let me go and I will reward you." And Wen P'eng, struck with pity and awe, put the beautiful creature back in the water.

The fish gave him in return a magic pearl, that brought ease and happiness to Wen P'eng and his mother but aroused the suspicions of their neighbour, a greedy and ruthless farmer. Accompanied by a gang of brutish farm-hands, the farmer and his wife descended on the widow when she was at home, alone.

"How is it," demanded the farmer's wife, "that you who were once so poor and miserable now live in such comfort? You have been sending your son out to steal! You are nothing but a pair of thieves, and we will have the law on you!"

Terrified out of her wits, the widow confessed that their prosperity was due to a magic pearl that increased in abundance everything that it touched.

Opposite: Paper-cut: boy with pearl.

"Where is this pearl?" said the farmer, as he and his gang ransacked the cottage. "Seize him!" they cried as Wen P'eng

appeared in the doorway; and they did so with such violence that Wen P'eng swallowed the pearl, which he was hiding in his mouth. He fainted away; and when he recovered he begged his mother to fetch him something to drink.

He drank and drank, but could not quench his thirst. He dragged himself to the river bank, and again drank greedily; but his body remained hot and feverish, great storm-clouds blew up, night came and the terrified mother saw that her dear son was slowly turning into a great dragon.

"My son, my son, do not leave me," she begged.

"Mother, mother, I am sorry to go, but I cannot stay," said the dragon, as a great gust of wind carried him up into the sky.

"Come back, come back," cried his mother.

The dragon turned sadly, and from his burning eyes tears fell slowly to the ground, and formed those lakes which lie today in the curves of the River Min.

Modern Chenille Ch'i Lin.

Dragon Thunder

In the spring, on the 15th day of the first month of the Chinese New Year, it was customary for the Chinese people to make a great din to wake up the dragons. They would construct huge dragons of bamboo, linen and paper and carry them round the streets and fields in procession, banging drums and letting off fire crackers, which exploded and flashed like the thunder and lightning of their celestial rain dragons.

Hong Kong rag dollies playing with a small papier maché lion mask.

In 1901, during the Boxer uprisings, the French writer Pierre Loti was serving as a young naval officer with the expeditionary force sent to relieve the foreign legations besieged in Peking. In his book 'The Last Days of Peking' he describes a village celebration.

"Suddenly two terrifying beasts appeared, one red, the other green. These enormous heraldic dragons were over twenty metres long; side by side they advanced towards us, heads reared, jaws open, with monstrous eyes, horns and claws.

"Over the heads of the crowd they raced along, like huge reptiles. But they were as light as air, being made of paper and cloth stretched over hoops. Each dragon was held aloft on poles carried by a dozen young men, who skilfully made its body twist and turn like a huge snake. A kind of ballet master pranced about in front of each dragon and stage-managed its monstrous evolutions.

"First of all the two dragons danced in front of us to the sound of gongs and flutes. Then they started to fight. The gong and cymbals clashed wildly. The dragons, locked in combat, twisting and turning, seized hold of each other, their long coils dragging in the dust. Then, leaping away, they reared up bristling with rage, while clouds of dust swirled up over the crowd, hiding the dragon-bearers from sight."

Engraving from Rev. J. Doolittle's monumental work "The Social Life of the Chinese", published in 1868.

蒺藜火毬以三枝六首鐵刀以藥藥團之中貫麻繩長一丈二尺外以紙并雜藥傳之又施鐵蒺藜八枚各有逆鬚放時燒鐵錐烙透令焰出　火藥法用硫黃一斤四兩焰硝二斤半炭末五兩瀝青二兩半乾漆二兩半搗為末竹茹一兩一分麻茹一分剪碎用桐油小油各二兩半蠟二兩半鎔汁和之傳用紙十二兩半麻一十兩黃丹一兩一分炭末半斤以瀝青二兩半黃蠟二兩鎔汁和合同塗之

右引火毬以紙為毬內實磚石俗可重三五斤藥包黃蠟瀝青炭末為泥同塗其物貫以麻繩凡將放火毬只先放此毬以準遠近

鐵嘴火鷂木身鐵觜尾為疎眼籠腹大口袋形微修竹火鷂編竹為疎眼籠腹大口袋形微修長外糊紙數重糊令黃色入火藥一斤在內加小卵石使其勢重束桿草三五斤為尾二物與毬同若賊來攻城欲以砲放之燔賊積聚及驚隊兵

Fire crackers and gunpowder

Did the Chinese invent gunpowder, for fireworks and for use in warfare? The question is debatable. Kenneth Allen in his book 'The Story of Gunpowder' states that "the Chinese seem to have used a form of 'Greek fire' or powder, which caused a flame, rather than gunpowder, which is an explosive . . . . . . They still knew very little, in the fifteenth century, about the manufacture of guns; and as late as 1618 Chinese guns were made under the supervision of the Jesuits . . . "

Dr. Joseph Needham (in 'The Grand Titration' and an article on 'China's Exploding Technology') thinks otherwise: "The oldest mention of any explosive substance known to man occurs in a Chinese Taoist text of the middle of the 9th century, where Taoist alchemists are strongly advised not to mix saltpetre, sulphur and a source of carbon with various other things like arsenic; because those who have done so have sometimes had the cottage explode where they were working . . .

"By the time of William the Conqueror rockets were flying through the Chinese air, with arrows on the end. At the same time also gunpowder, probably very low in nitrate, was put in bombs which were thrown from trebuchets—a kind of catapult. Just a bit later we get the first printed formulae for gunpowder in any civilisation."

As to metal-barrelled guns or cannons, Dr. Needham does not rate highly any claims that these were invented in the West; for the natural bamboo tubes existed in the East and not in the West.

A page from the Wu Ching Tsung Yao of AD1044, showing the earliest formula for gunpowder in any civilisation (from Joseph Needham: Hand and Brain in China).

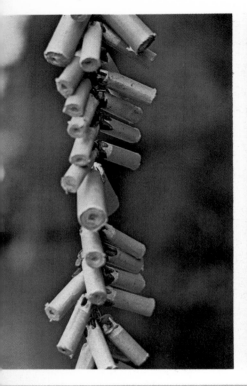

He points out that the first dated cannon are all Chinese, from the 1360s onwards, which is some half a century earlier than the oldest dated ones in the West; but he concedes that this does not prove the point of actual origin.

However that may be, it is certain that the Chinese love letting off fire crackers. As the Reverend Father Huc says, writing of his travels through China in the 1840s, every occasion is an excuse for fireworks: births, weddings, funerals, official receptions, informal parties, theatrical shows, religious feast-days, secular holidays. Great bunches of fire crackers hanging on bamboo poles explode; dragons and other mythical creatures spit fire through every pore; multi-coloured rockets burst in the sky, while in plates on the ground flying suns whizz round and round and then shoot up into the air amidst a cascade of pretty blue sparklets. Even in the poorest hamlet lacking the barest necessities of life, says Father Huc, one is sure to find someone selling fireworks and pumpkin seeds.

Until recent times making fireworks was a cottage industry, everything being done by hand in small family undertakings. Today however fireworks are manufactured in large factories. The town of Linyang, in the province of Hunan, is one of the main centres: it has more than 5,000 people, in nine large factories, engaged in producing them. All the processes are mechanised, and even more elaborate fireworks are being designed, mostly for grand displays: larger and more dazzling

Opposite, top left: String of Chinese fire crackers.

Opposite, top right: Fireworks at night.

Above left: Fireworks on display in Peking shop.

Above right: More fireworks for sale.

Opposite, below: Children in Sports Stadium holding flash cards.

dragons, peacocks, flying suns and flights of pretty butterflies. There are smaller and more amusing motifs, too, such as the 'Happy Family Party Firework', which when lit first makes a noise as of people laughing, then changes to loud clapping, and finally bursts into a rainbow shower of bright colours, symbolising family happiness.

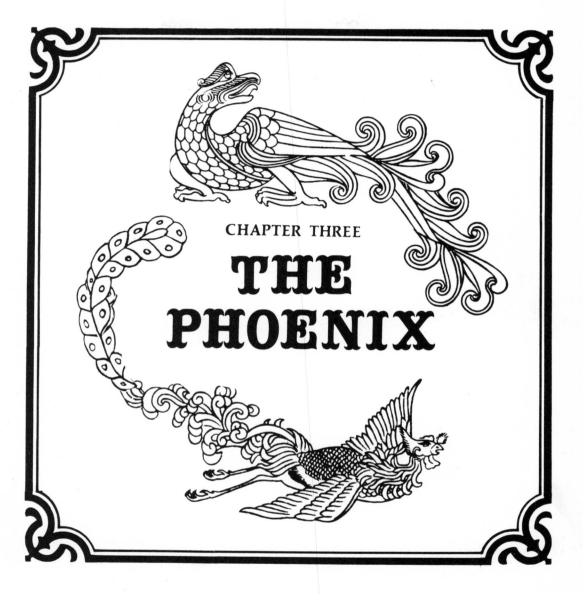

CHAPTER THREE

THE PHOENIX

*In which an English Phoenix tells
of his Chinese relatives, of a Chinese boy's
journey to the Western Paradise, and of how
he caught and tamed a golden Phoenix. And in which
is related why Chinese lions delight in dancing,
and the wickedness and magical feats of the
Monkey King are celebrated.*

All devoted readers of E. Nesbit's books will know that some time in July 1903, in London, a Phoenix was born. It was hatched out in the basement of No. 18 Camden Terrace, where four children —Anthea, Jane, Cyril and Robert—were burning eucalyptus oil and camphor on the nursery fire. The day before they had found a stone egg, rolled up in an old carpet; and Robert accidentally knocked it off the mantelpiece on to the red-hot heart of the fire. The egg burst in two, and out of it came a flame-coloured bird which flew around the room, then settled on the fender to cool off.

The Phoenix's conversation was entertaining and instructive, like school prizes are said to be. It discussed many topics with the children—but alas it never mentioned its Chinese relatives. Yet it

The Scroll: feeding sacred mushrooms to a phoenix. The teapot-shaped musical instrument with bamboo reeds sounds something like pan pipes.

Below: modern Chenille monkeys.

is easy to imagine what the London phoenix's comments on them would have been:

"Ah yes, the Feng Huang—my very distant relatives. Very ancient and fabulous, however. They do not, like me, reside in the wilderness, which is a large quiet place with very little really good society; nor have they acquired, as I have, the habit of burning themselves every 500 years or so on a pile of sweet-smelling wood, and rising again from the ashes. Like rocs and all respectable birds they lay eggs, but they are—or so I've been told—infertile things: just solid lumps of gold, not delicate, translucent yellow eggs with a living yolk of pale fire, like mine.

"Long ago, in the time of the ancient Egyptians and the Phoenicians, a train of camels came wandering through my

desert, and in their packs were rolls of delicate silks embroidered or painted with pictures of my Chinese relative Feng Huang. They are not, like me, of the race of eagles, but rather of the hen or pheasant family. They stand quite six feet tall, and have a brilliant plumage of many colours. They feed on bamboo seeds, live mainly in paulownia woods but have been seen in many other parts of China. They are birds of high noon and summer days. In olden times they graced the imperial courts of the great Empresses of the Middle Kingdom, yet never failed to appear at the weddings of even the humblest Chinese peasants . . . . . ."

The London phoenix paused a moment, as if lost in reverie. Then it went on:

"You know the story of Jack and the Beanstalk, of course? And the one about the goose that laid the golden eggs? And you remember my telling you that my Chinese relative lays eggs of solid gold? There's a story about this too.

A CHINESE STORY
The Phoenix who laid the Golden Eggs

Long ago there lived in China a boy who was always so kind and happy that his friends and neighbours gave him a nickname which in Chinese means something like 'Happy-Hopeful'.

Now Happy-Hopeful wanted to marry the pretty young girl who lived next door. "Not a hope," said her mother. "I'm looking for a son-in-law with rather better prospects. I'll consent if you bring me three hairs from the head of Buddha."

"Right!" said Happy-Hopeful, and he set off the next day for the far-distant Western Paradise, his only companion a little tame robin perched on his shoulder. He travelled up hill and down dale, and on his way he met many unfortunate people. He always spoke to them courteously and promised to help them if ever he reached Buddha's throne.

At long last he came to the doors of Paradise, and there he could see one of Buddha's favourite lime-trees spreading out over the heavens its huge canopy of green leaves. But two powerful monks guarded the entrance. "No entry," they said, and their voices rolled like thunder.

Just then, up flew the little robin, chirping gaily, and circled round the monk's heads.

"What a pretty little bird," said the gatekeepers; and in the moment their attention was distracted Happy-Hopeful slipped

past them and raced up to the golden throne where Buddha was sitting, meditating on his next re-incarnation, while around him a great swelling chant of prayer went surging up.

"I have come to beg three golden hairs from your head," shouted Happy-Hopeful, trying in vain to make himself heard. Then, catching hold of Buddha's robe, he started to haul himself up till he reached Buddha's shoulder, and found himself surrounded by the bright, gleaming locks which covered Buddha's chest and back.

Happy-Hopeful steadied himself, then with a quick yank he pulled out three long, fine, golden hairs.

"Aie, aie, what's that biting me?" cried Buddha. Happy-Hopeful loosed his hold, slid to the ground, and quick as a flash he reached the gates, called to his friend the robin and set off towards home.

On his way back, thanks to the magic power of Buddha's hair he was able to help all those who had helped him on his way. And he also caught a golden, fiery phoenix. Then, three years to the day after setting out, he came back to his own village and presented the three golden hairs to his beloved's mother.

Some time after the wedding, one day when Happy-Hopeful was away from home, his mother-in-law came nosing round.

"How do you manage to feed that great fiery bird?" she asked.

"Oh, it's quite easy," said her guileless daughter. "Each morning Happy-Hopeful gives it a little rice from its special store, then sings it this little song:

Golden phoenix, Queen of birds, my fabulous treasure,

Give me health, give me wealth, and eggs in good measure.

"And then the phoenix lays two golden eggs."

"My darling girl, just lend her to me for a little while," said the old woman. "I'll take great care of her and bring her back before your husband returns."

She rushed home and started singing the magic incantation over and over again, until she was dizzy from counting. As for the poor phoenix, she was quite exhausted from laying so many golden eggs. Suddenly she toppled over on her back and lay there quite dead.

And what did the greedy old woman do then? "Well," she thought, "I might as well make something out of a bad job"; so she set about cooking and then eating the beautiful golden bird. But gold is indigestible. She choked and died.

Happy-Hopeful came home and buried his mother-in-law and what remained of the bird.

Some time later there appeared over the grave of the phoenix a green shoot. Happy-Hopeful tended it carefully till it grew into a

Below: Cantonese lions in Gerrard Street, London, at the time of the Chinese New Year.

beautiful tree, covered with sweet-scented white flowers. The petals dropped, and pretty, round green fruit appeared which slowly ripened into a crop of glowing, luscious, golden oranges.

"That," said the London Phoenix, "is the end of my story about my Chinese relative. But long, long afterwards, among the cargoes of tea, silk, wallpaper, porcelain, lacquered chests and other exotic luxuries brought to England by the 'China Clippers', were baskets of these golden fruits; and they would be sold to the gallants of King Charles II's court, as they flocked to the Drury Lane theatres, by Nell Gwynne and other pretty sellers crying "Buy, buy my sweet China oranges!"

Dancing Lions and Monkeys

From the world of myth and legend, of fabulous creatures and heroic feats, we come back to reality. The scroll is damaged, but we can discern that the children are imitating the jolly feats of professional lion dancers; for in China the lion readily assumes a character that recalls our pantomine horse. At certain festivals street dancers would don a bewhiskered mask and drape a loose, baggy cloth over their bodies; then caper down the highway to the vast delight of the children gathered round them.

The rows of ferocious, fantastic stone lions that stand guard over the entrances to royal tombs and over princely gateways in China are as unreal in their fashion as the pantomine lions. For while tigers and other kinds of wild cats live in the mountains of

Peking Lion Dance, painted by a Chinese child.

A Peking Lion dancing: from a 19th century folk print.

Southern China, no lions do. Pictures and carvings of lions came to China from India at the same time as the Buddhist religion, and it was hoped that these terrifying images would help to keep evil spirits away. At times of plague or other calamity temple priests would assume the lion's role themselves, putting on masks and a great pantomine act of chasing away the wicked devils.

Monkeys are popular too. They are wicked, but clever; so they get away with it. The King of the Monkeys can change his shape at will and whizz through the air like an oriental Superman. He created havoc among the gods, drinking too much at a festival in his honour for having slain a monster; stealing the register of judgements from hell and deleting his own and all other monkeys' names; and eating all the Peaches of Immortality in the heavenly Peach Garden he was supposed to superintend. He even tried conclusions with the Buddha, who eventually shut him up in a magic mountain—from which he was later released to assist in the pilgrimage to the Western Paradise to fetch authentic versions of the Buddha's teachings.

The pranks of the Monkey King were published over 400 years ago and have been read with equal enchantment by children and grown-ups ever since. The King of the Monkeys has also been immensely popular as a stage character. The role of the Monkey King gives enormous scope to the acrobatic talents of the actors who play in the special form of entertainment—part pantomine, part musical comedy, part drama—which is known as the Peking Opera.

Illustration from a modern, popular edition of "Monkey, a Journey to the West" by Wu Ch'eng-en, first published in the 16th century.

唐僧又急忙披

CHAPTER FOUR

CHINESE GAMES

*Of divers Chinese games: Of kicking
the Foot Ball, and the Chien-Tzu; of spinning
tops and yo-yos, and the ingenuity of the Chinese in
constructing toys of all kinds. Of kites and
their uses, and the hazards of man-
lifting kites; of children's skipping
games, and the Hop Scotch.*

Kicking the Chien-Tzu and playing football

Opposite: An early 20th century Chinese doll made for export. The boy is kicking a Chien-Tzu — a shuttlecock made from feathers poked through the hole in a Chinese coin and sewn into a tiny leather bag.

On one side of the boys doing the lion dance is a little boy in red, whom we have already seen dancing: here he is kicking a ball in the air. On the other side, there he is again, this time kicking a feathered shuttlecock with the heel of his shoe.

Two other boys are waiting to kick the ball in their turn. They are not practising football as we know it, but a much slower game in which the ball has to be kicked from one person to the next without ever falling to the ground.

This ancient form of Chinese football became very popular at the Japanese court in the 7th century, and it has survived there as an aristocratic pastime till quite recent times, so we do know how it is played. The ball is made of two circles of deerskin sewn together, the seams forming a slight waist round the middle. Four, six or eight people can play; and the ground is a 40 ft. square. Japanese devotees wear ceremonial dress and black lacquered platform shoes.

The Scroll: kicking the Chien-Tzu with the sole of the feet.

In 1881 the Emperor Meiji, who was very fond of the game,

Above: Polo.

Below: Chinese tops, drawn by Kwok Siu Wing.

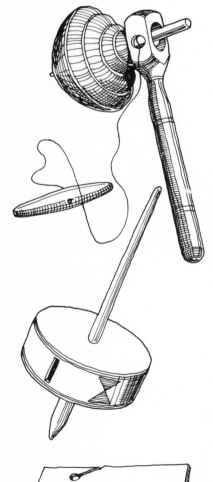

founded the 'Kemari' Preservation Society with headquarters at Kyoto. The game is played there five times a year, with occasional extra performances for distinguished guests paying state visits to Japan.

Polo as played in China over 1,000 years ago has also been preserved unchanged in Japan. The game calls for skilful horsemanship and physical toughness; but it is nothing compared with the original wild ball games played by the nomadic herdsmen of Mongolia who became, through their repeated invasions, an integral part of Chinese history.

Team games, with the exception perhaps of the Tug-of-War, have not until quite recently been a popular form of recreation in China. Individual skill and dexterity was much more encouraged, whether for flying a kite, or kicking a Chien-Tzu.

The Chien-Tzu is made quite simply from a Chinese coin wrapped up in a bit of rag or very soft leather, and flight feathers which are secured by poking a small length of goose quill through the hole in the middle of the coin. Small discs of cardboard, or even seed pods, can be used instead of money. The object is to keep this shuttlecock in the air as long as possible, always catching it on the heel of the foot. Is it surprising that with the reflexes of generation after generation trained in this way the young people of China today should achieve such outstanding success as gymnasts and at ping-pong?

Tops—Diabolos—Yoyos

The same dexterity—part natural, part acquired by diligent practice—characterises the way Chinese children handle such toys as tops, yoyos, diabolos.

Chinese tops are of many kinds. Children play with them in winter mostly, spinning them with whips on the frozen ground. In Korea they are made of hard-wood; but further south often of lotus seed-pods, through which iron spindles are driven like nails. A cord is twined round the spindle and pulled sharply to set the top in motion. Skilful players can spin this top on a slender branch or even a wire.

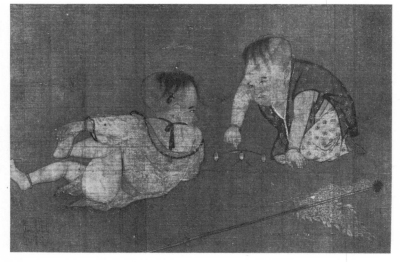

Everyone plays ping-pong in China today, but it is not a Chinese invention. It was launched on the world in 1901, under the name of Table Tennis or Gossamer, by Mr Walter Hamley, owner of the world-famous London toyshop.

Two boys playing with a balancing top made from acorns. A 12th or 13th century Sung Dynasty painting, now in the Museum of Fine Arts, Boston (John Ware Willard Fund).

Country people also use conch shells, grinding the pointed heads flat and the tips round: then they wind a cord round them and spin them on a mat tray—two or three tops togather, the one which is knocked off the tray being the loser.

Small children often make tiny tops of acorns, with a bamboo spindle: these they can spin with their fingers. Boys also play a game in which they themselves are a kind of top. A boy draws a circle on the ground, stands inside, folds his arms with one hand clutching one of his ears. Then he twirls himself around and sees how many turns he can make before he accidentally steps outside the circle.

Of course the Chinese have humming tops too—and indeed humming diabolos. The humming quality had the advantage, from the street pedlar's point of view, of helping him attract customers. A book published in France in 1812, 'La Chine en Miniature', has an engraving showing a pedlar doing just this: it is the first known illustration in the West of this very Chinese toy, and may well have started the diabolo craze which swept through France shortly afterwards.

Periodic crazes have also characterised the history of the yoyo (also called the bandalore or the Prince of Wales's quiz) since it reached Europe from China in the 18th century. Its high-water mark of popularity came in the late 20s and early 30s of this century: in 1932 the American firm of Louis Marx after copyrighting the name 'yoyo' sold 100,000,000 of them.

On a higher plane of manipulative, and still more of manufacturing skill, soars the Chinese invention of the kite, with a history long and venerable enough to require a section of its own.

Kite-flying

On 19th October, 1782 a vast crowd assembled in Paris to watch the first man to fly up into the sky. A few days before, there had been proof that it was possible to breathe in the atmosphere above the earth: for attached to the hot-air balloon made by the Montgolfier brothers a duck, a hen, and a sheep had made the ascent and returned to earth safely. It was now proposed to make a further trial with a condemned prisoner, but at the last moment a young nobleman, Pilatre de Rosier, stepped forward, saying to King Louis: "It is not fit that the first man to fly should be a

Early Chinese kites were simple rectangles. Today, Chinese craftsmen make kites for export in many beautiful shapes and colours.

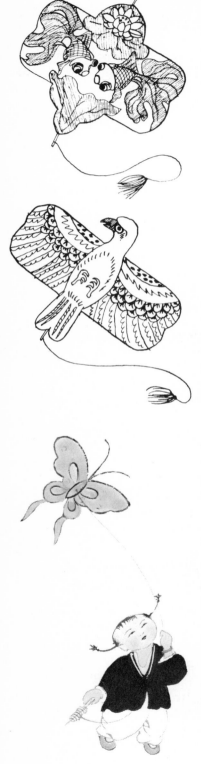

low-born gaolbird. Allow me, Sire, to take his place." And up he sailed to 324 feet, staying airborne for nine long minutes. A week or so later, he and the Marquis d'Arlandes daringly cut the tow-rope and to the astonishment of everyone sailed safely over Paris, as free as the birds which men had watched with wonder and envy since the legendary times of Daedalus and Icarus.

Yet were these gallant young French noblemen the first to fly? They were not; for far away in the Celestial Empire of the East tipsy Chinamen and condemned prisoners had for centuries been sent hurtling into the sky, attached to huge man-lifting kites made of silk and bamboo. Marco Polo is our witness:

"When any ship must go on a voyage, they prove whether its business will go well or ill on that voyage. The men of the ship will have a hurdle, that is a grating, of withies; and at each corner and side of the hurdle will be tied a cord, so that there will be eight cords, and they will all be tied at the other end with a long rope. Then they will find someone stupid or drunken and will bind him on the hurdle. This is done when a strong wind prevails: they set up the hurdle opposite the wind, and the wind lifts the hurdle and carries it into the sky, while the men hold on by the long rope.

"If while it is in the air the hurdle leans towards the way of the wind, they pull the rope to them a little and then the hurdle is set upright, and they let out some rope and the hurdle rises. And if it leans down again they pull the rope by so much till the hurdle is set up and rises, and they let out some rope . . .

"The proof is made in this way: if the hurdle going straight up makes for the sky, they say that the ship will make a quick and prosperous voyage; and all the merchants run together to her for the sake of sailing with her. But if the hurdle has not been able to go up, no merchant will be willing to enter that ship, and she stays in port that year."

Man-lifting kites were not only used for forecasting the weather and for foretelling good or bad luck as Marco Polo tells us: they also served as observation posts in military operations.

Silk has been produced in China for nearly 5,000 years; paper for over 2,000 years; and bamboo, which can be put to so many different uses, is native to China. All the materials for making kites have therefore been available in China long before they were in other parts of the world; so it is highly probable that the Chinese were the first to make them. Dr. Joseph Needham suggests that the first kite may have been a farmer's hat held by a string. Clive Hart, in his authoritative history of kites, hazards the view that the idea may have come from the sight of pennons or banners streaming out in the wind, or perhaps even of the sail of a boat blowing away while it was being hauled down.

Whatever the distant origins of kites, as long ago as 200 BC General Han Hsin is said to have flown a kite over the walls of a city he was besieging so that he could calculate (by trigonometry) the required length of the tunnel he was secretly digging and through which his soldiers would later emerge behind the enemy fortifications. Another general, hemmed in and threatened with annihilation, is reported to have had the ingenious idea of scaring his enemies away by flying over their tents at dead of night musical kites fitted with harp-like strings which whistled in the wind. Musical kites were also used for non-military purposes, such as scaring the birds from the fields, and for protecting houses at night from robbers and evil spirits.

It does not appear, however, that kites were flown for fun in China until some time in the 10th century, and then only in the autumn on a special kite-flying day, the 9th day of the 9th month. This 'Festival of the Ascension' was connected with the scholarly Civil Service examinations which took place a few weeks before. Everyone went up into the hills with bottles of chrysanthemum wine and special picnic foods—and also their kites. The higher your kite flew, the better your hopes for a good place in the exams would be. And even if your future looked bleak you could at least have a good fight with a neighbour's kite. Men and boys would strengthen and sharpen the silk strings of their kites by dipping them in fish glue and then in powdered glass or porcelain: they would then engage in great fights, trying to cut through their rivals' kite-strings.

Fighting kites and the earlier practical, man-lifting kites appear to have been rectangular in shape; but during the 18th and 19th centuries Chinese kites became more and more complicated and beautiful: kites with wings like birds or insects, and the spectacular dragon or centipede kite of circular discs joined by two or more lines—a full 60 feet long, and requiring a whole team of men to launch and fly it.

The skill and ingenuity of the Chinese kite-makers spread abroad to their neighbours in Japan, Korea, Thailand, Polynesia and Tibet. Lobsang Rampa, in his book 'The Third Eye', has a terrifying account of how a party of Buddhist monks, sent out on an expedition to gather medicinal herbs in the Himalayas, would use kites for sport at the risk of their lives.

On a high, bleak plateau, at certain times of day the winds from the valley below would rush up through a narrow crevice in the rocks at tremendous speeds. In a box-shaped kite which they had constructed from silk and wood back at the lamasery the monks would launch themselves straight up into the airstream and rise thousands of feet above the valley below—their robes flapping in the wind, their feet on a narrow pole, their arms linked over a crossbar, while a team of monks and horses struggled to hold down the twisting, swaying kite. Not unexpectedly, one or two of the most daring monks lost their grip, slipped and hurtled to their deaths on the rocks below.

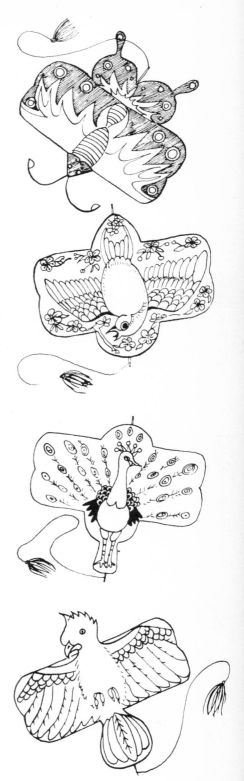

Opposite: A blob or two of sun-dried clay, some odds and ends of coiled wire springs, and a handful of feathers make this pretty "flutter bird".

Below: Spinning top, cricket cages and tiny baskets and boxes, made from bamboo or split straws. Cricket-keeping is said to date back to the time of the T'ang emperor T'ien Po (742—755 AD) at whose court highborn ladies reared crickets to sing, and to fight for high stakes.

Something from Nothing

However sophisticated in their ultimate development, kites are basically simple things: here, as so often, the Chinese have shown the world how things useful, beautiful, and amusing can be made out of practically nothing—except ingenuity. And the smaller the scale, very often, the greater the ingenuity and the higher the fantasy.

Thus Juliet Bredon, writing sixty years ago of a Peking street trader's ware: "A group of little figures made of paper and standing on horse hairs are made to dance on a brass tray by a light tap on the edge. A flock of geese fly up and down a thread by loosening or tightening the bent bamboo attached to it. Butterflies of paper flutter on light osier twigs. Always the cheapest materials are used—paper, bamboo, straw, clay or bits of wood or feathers."

A balancing trick cyclist, made from scrap metal, brightly coloured bits of rag, and clay.

Below: Grasshopper made from plaited palm-leaf.

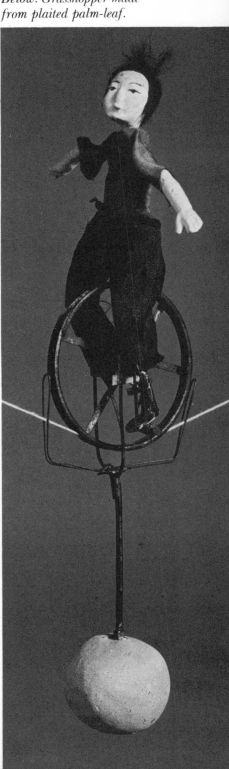

To make the body of a palm-leaf grasshopper, you cut the palm-leaf in strips, plait them tightly round the spine of the leaf, and then poke thin strips of leaf spine into the main plait to form legs, antennae and wings. Drawing by Chan Hung Yue.

If Chinese children have shared in these skills, that does not in itself make them exceptional. Throughout the ages, until mass production in factories, children have had to invent their playthings out of nothing. All the toys in Breughel's 16th century paintings of children at play are toys they could devise themselves. But where industrialisation has been a late-comer, ingenuity applied to simple things has lasted longer. And so with China: three students, visiting London in 1973, recounted how as boys

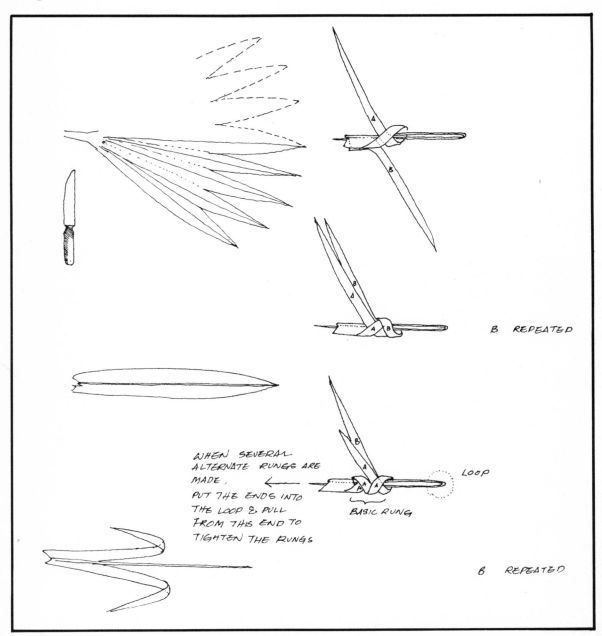

B REPEATED

WHEN SEVERAL ALTERNATE RUNGS ARE MADE, ← PUT THE ENDS INTO THE LOOP & PULL FROM THIS END TO TIGHTEN THE RUNGS

LOOP

BASIC RUNG

B REPEATED

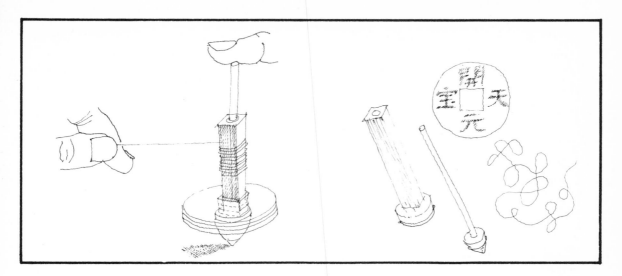

they had made whizzing propellors, water squirts and popguns out of bits of bamboo; folded paper to make heavy flick darts; and collected snail shells, peas and fruit stones for use as counters in complicated games of chance, mostly invented by themselves. Other popular pastimes were shadow boxing and walking on stilts; or (for country dwellers) catching crickets by poking into bushes sticks of bamboo tipped with a black, gluey substance.

Above: This drawing by Chan Hung Yue shows how he made spinning tops, when he was a boy, from old Chinese "cash" coins, matchsticks glued together and a lollipop stick.

Below: Woven palm-leaf cow.

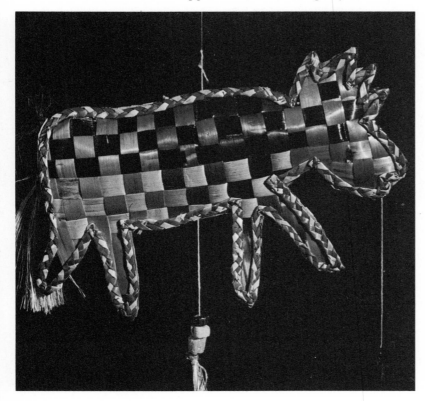

O-U-T SPELLS OUT

One, two, three

And an old cow's eye

Now she's blind

She'll surely die

I'll let you have

The old cow skin

And a melon too

All for you

But if you can't pay

Then we all say

Out you must go.

Peking Nursery Rhyme

CHINESE SKIPPING

Round about 1965 a form of skipping known as 'Chinese skipping' became very popular in England. Instead of a rope, a length of elastic was used, or quantities of elastic bands looped together. A seven-year-old English girl, Anita Little, explains how it is done:

CHAPTER 1
ALL ABOUT ELASTIC

When you get your piece of elastic you tie a special knot. You get two friends and you put one end of the elastic round one person and the other end round the other person. Then they stand apart. Then I do the following jumps like tinker in tinker over out which we call ordinaries. And from the out side you jump right over the elastic saying tinker over tinker in out which we call opposites.

CHAPTER 2
RULES FOR BEING OUT

On elastic if you tread on the elastic you would be out. And if you caught your heel and buckle in the elastic you would be out. And if you missed out a jump you would be out. And if you did the jump wrong you would be out.

CHAPTER 3
POSITION OF ELASTIC

First you put it on your ankle, Then you put it round your knees, Then you put it round your hip.

This little frog has two eyes,

Four legs,

One mouth, no tail,

Says croak, croak and

Plops into the water.

These little frogs have four eyes,

Eight legs,

Two mouths, no tails,

Say croak, croak and

Plop into the water.

etc.

Traditional Chinese Nursery Rhyme

My little baby, little boy blue,
Is as sweet as sugar and
Cinnamon too;
Isn't this precious darling of
ours Sweeter than dates and
cinnamon flowers?

Peking Nursery Rhyme

Opposite, top: Snake of folded
paper.
Opposite, below: Early 20th
century composition and rag
doll made for export, with set
of wooden toy cooking pots
and pans.

"Tinker, tailor, soldier,
sailor." On a baby's first
birthday in China it was the
custom to place him in the
centre of a selection of articles
representing different
professions, and to wait and
see which one he would stretch
out to clutch in his little fist.
For this "Cha-Chou" ceremony
he would wear his new
"Hundred Families"
patchwork coat and shoes
embroidered with a tiger's face
to ward off evil spirits. The
doll in this picture was made
by Ruby Ting in Hong Kong.

ENGLISH 'PIGGIES' GO TO
MARKET, BUT CHINESE
COWS EAT GRASS.

This little cow eats grass,
This little cow eats hay,
This little cow drinks water,
This little cow runs away,

This little cow does nothing,
But just lies down all day,
We'll whip her, let's whip her,
let's whip her.

Traditional Chinese Nursery Rhyme

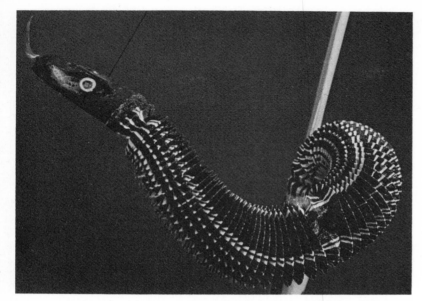

THE TOYMAN'S SONG

SMILEY girley, losy boy,
S'posey makee buy my toy;
Littee devilos make of clay,
Awful snakey clawley 'way,
Glate black spider, eyes all led,
Dlagons fit to scaree dead.
Dis de sortey plitty toy
Sell to littee China-boy.

From: Pidgin English Sing-Song,
published in 1897.

ROUND AND ROUND
THE GARDEN.

This little lady drinks wine,
This little lady warms it,
This little lady brings dishes
    of salt vegetables,
This little lady serves food,
And this little lady passes the plates
    round and round and
    round . . . . . .
And now that all the company
    have arrived, we will play at
    Fists and Finger, Guess What
    and other merry feats.

Peking Nursery Rhyme

Chinese children, like all children, play at Cat's Cradle

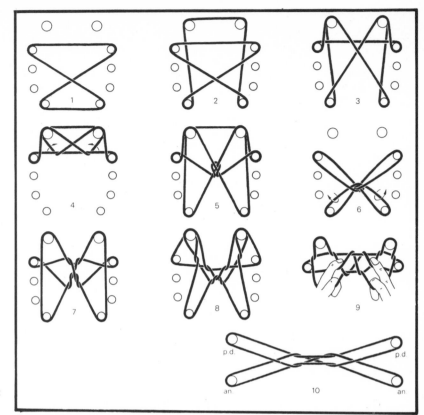

and at a finger guessing game: Scissors (two fingers), paper (open hand), stone (closed fist). Drawing by Kwok Siu Wing.

Scissors cut paper

Stone breaks scissors.

Paper wraps stone

CHAPTER FIVE

PUZZLES AND GAMES

*Of games and puzzles exercising
the mind: Of Chinese Chess, and the game
known as Go; of ladies' games, especially Spillikins
and Mah-Jong; of Tangrams and other Puzzles,
with scholarly observations on their origins
and probable purposes, and their
survival through the centuries.*

Chess (Hsiang-Ch'i) and Go (Wei-Ch'i)

Contrary to popular belief, chess did not originate in China but in India. Initially, as 'Shaturanga', it took the form of a miniature battle played on a board of 64 squares between four armies each having infantry, cavalry, elephants and boatmen and being commanded by a Rajah. Later the four players became two only, there were changes in the moves, and the true ancestor of modern chess (Shatranj) was evolved.

From India the game spread, in about the 7th century AD, both westwards to Persia and eastwards to China (some authorities give a considerably earlier date for its emergence in China). In the Chinese version (Hsiang-Ch'i) each army has a fortress from within which the general and his mandarins direct the operations of their elephants, horsemen, infantry, cannon and war-chariots, with the object of taking the enemy fortress by storm. Across the

Paper chessboard and chessmen.

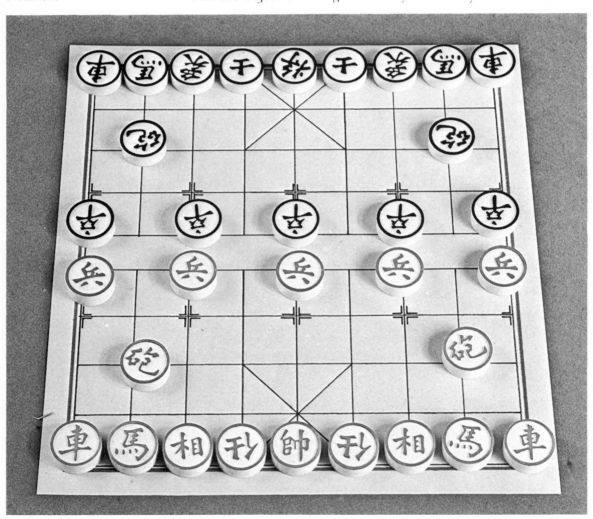

centre of the board is a space one square wide known as 'the river', which the elephants cannot cross. The pieces are placed on the intersections of the lines on the board, not on the spaces as in Western chess.

The chessmen, despite their engagingly aggressive names, are much less picturesque than many of those developed in the west, or even than standard modern chessmen. They are distinguished not by size and shape, being all uniform circular discs, but by having their ranks inscribed on the upper face—in red for one side, black for the other. The moves of some of the pieces correspond with those of pieces in modern international chess.

Go

Chess in China has traditionally been the game of the middle and lower classes, and played for small stakes. The intelligentsia have rather despised it, preferring the older and more difficult game of Wei-Ch'i ('Go' in the Japanese version). This has a much bigger board than chess (18 × 18 squares), and each player has some 200 uniform pieces, known as 'tze', which they place in turn on the intersections of the squares. Briefly, the object is to surround groups of the enemy forces with troops of your own, thereby eliminating them.

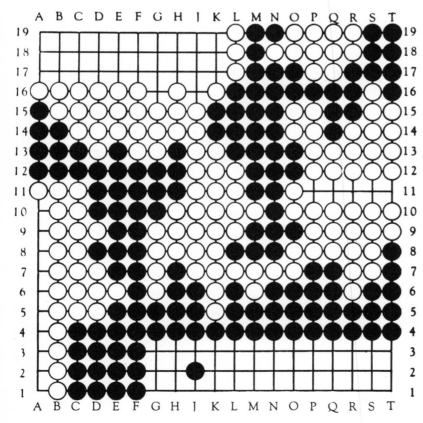

The economical Chinese did not generally use the elaborate, lacquered Go sets favoured by the Japanese players. Two bowls for the black and white counters and a printed paper board were sufficient.

The Scroll: Playing Go in the garden.

Wei-Ch'i is mentioned in Chinese literature as far back as the 7th century BC. Confucius thought it good intellectual exercise for the idle rich. Skill at the game could be a strong recommendation for promotion at work; and Edward Falkener, in his book on 'Games Ancient and Oriental' (1892) quotes the British Consul in China as saying: "Skill in Wei-Ch'i implies the astuteness and versatility so prized amongst the Chinese. They could hardly believe a man to play Wei-Ch'i well and yet be possessed of only indifferent abilities as a practical man of the world." It is no surprise therefore to find two of the boys in our 'Hundred Sons' scroll busily engaged at the game.

In recent years Wei-Ch'i sets have not been manufactured in China, as they are thought to be time-wasting and to encourage gambling—a national vice in the old China. Not so in Japan, where 'Go'—continues to flourish as it has done ever since, long ago, the Japanese learnt it from the Chinese.

In the Boston Museum of Fine Arts there is a hand scroll depicting the adventures of Kibi in China. Kibi was one of several eminent Japanese statesmen who visited the court of the T'ang Emperor during the 7th century AD. The story goes that the Chinese, jealous of his wisdom, subjected him to a series of demanding tests, including a contest at 'Go'.

On the right of the picture Kibi sits at the board, facing a visibly despondent Chinese team. A Chinese supporter is peering underneath the board, suspecting that a 'Go' piece is missing. So it is: Kibi has swallowed it.

On the left of the picture we see Kibi in his underwear while the Chinese, who have given him a purge, examine his excrement. In vain: Kibi by a magic trick has succeeded in retaining the missing piece in his stomach.

Edward Lasker, the American chess master, writing in 1932 said: "I am convinced that 'Go' will gradually share with chess the leading position among intellectual games in the occident, just as it has reigned supreme in the orient for the last three thousand years." To achieve this distinction it still has some way to Go; but its popularity is certainly on the increase not only in America, but in Britain and other European countries too. Perhaps it is preoccupying Bobby Fischer?

Parlour Games

'Go' may be thought, without disparagement to the ladies, to require a masculine mind. Chinese chess, on the other hand, in

Chinese ladies playing cards: an early 19th century Chinese genre painting for the European market. The Royal Pavilion, Brighton.

the opinion of Edward Falkener demanded above all "a quick eye and ready wit." "Indeed," he adds, "owing to the lightness and brilliancy which distinguish the game, by comparison with the solidity of ordinary chess, it might with great propriety be called 'Ladies' Chess."

Playing Cards

Female tastes too, according to one Chinese source, were responsible for the emergence of playing cards in China. This ascribes their invention to the need of the Emperor Seun-ho, in 1120 AD, to find a diversion for his concubines. The claim is contested by other nations; but since the Chinese were the first manufacturers of paper, and the first to use a paper currency, it is very reasonable to suppose that playing cards too owe their origin to this inventive race of gamblers.

Spillikins

If spillikins were not invented for ladies they were, in their more recent history, gratefully adopted by them. Let us observe, for example, the ladies of Queen Victoria's court at Windsor, whiling away the long evenings of winter, 1845. From a pretty little box, the delicately carved ivory spillikins were gathered together in a loosely-held bundle, then allowed to fall higgledy-piggledy on to the table. With an elegant display of lace, jewels and lily-white hands each player in turn tried to lift up with her finger-tips, or

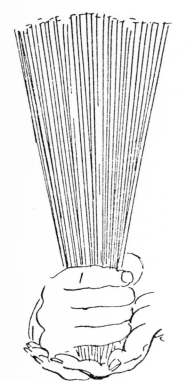

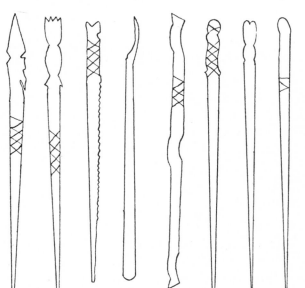

Telling fortunes with fifty dried yarrow stalks or small wooden sticks. The pattern they make when dropped can be interpreted, like that of tea-leaves in a cup.

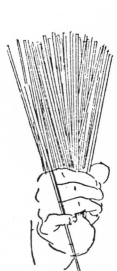

with two special hooks, a single spillikin—without touching or moving any of the others in the pile. The ends of the 30 or so tiny sticks which make up a set were carved in the shape of daggers, crosses, lances or swords; and each had an allotted value.

How surprised—and perhaps amused—these ladies would have been to learn that this trifling game had been played in earnest for thousands of years in far-away China—not as a test of skill and dexterity, but in an attempt to foresee the future.

In games involving skill and judgment, whether Western or Eastern (Chess, Go, Mah-Jong) two human beings pit their wits against each other. They may be ill-matched, but in their efforts to see and forestall their opponent's plans each must work within the limits set by human intelligence and ingenuity. But the evidence of counters, dice and marked stones found in ancient tombs and other excavations in Mesopotamia, India and the Far East suggests to some archaeologists that many games of chance were in their origins attempts at divination. Man diced not with another man but with Fate, with the gods.

Chinese playing cards are long and narrow.

"Spillikins", "Pick up Sticks", "Jack Straws" or "Mikado". Each little stick or shape has a different value.

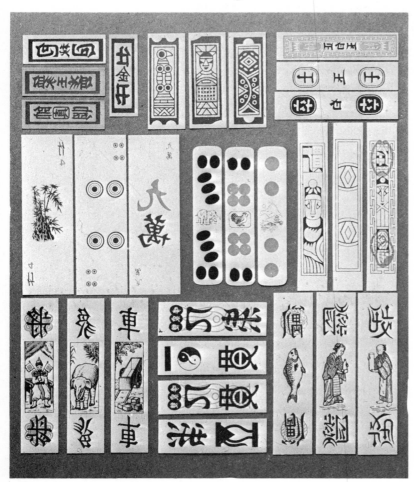

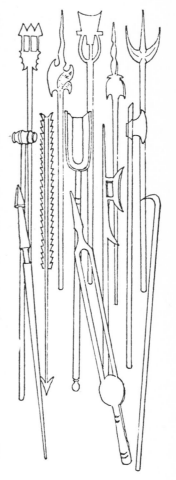

So, perhaps, with spillikins. Stewart Culin, in his book 'Games of the Orient' (published in 1895) advances the theory that spillikins may have evolved from the practice of casting lots; or foretelling how the hunt would go by holding in the hand a quiver of arrows, letting them fall to the ground, and interpreting the pattern they made there. Indeed, until fairly recently street fortune-tellers in many parts of the Far East used little bundles of sticks in just this way.

Perhaps, too, the name 'Jackstraws', by which the game of spillikins is known in Ireland and the U.S.A., relates to the way country children all over Europe used to cast lots by drawing the shortest straw from a little bunch held in the fist.

Mah-Jong

Last among our 'ladies' games is a late Chinese invention—not indeed exclusive to ladies, but for decades the darling of their salons. Mah Jong is a complex and sophisticated game, with a flavour of poker and rummy on a base of dominoes. In Peking it is called Matchang, meaning 'sparrow'—perhaps because the clicking sound of the pieces as they made contact was thought to resemble the chirruping of sparrows.

The invention of Mah Jong has been attributed (cf. the 'Diction-naire des Jeux', ed. Claude Tchou, Paris 1964) to Hung Hsiu-ch'üan, the fanatical instigator of the T'ai P'ing revolt at Nanking in 1860, who proclaimed himself Emperor and King of Heaven. The attribution is questionable; but Hung Hsiu-ch'üan was in all probability the figurehead of one of the most powerful secret societies in China, the 'Hong' or 'Triade', and the game itself appears to have hidden, symbolic links with the secret codes of the Hong society.

After about 1900 the popularity of Mah Jong spread like wildfire through upper and middle class China. From China it invaded American society, from America British. The craze lacked staying power, however; by 1935 it had burnt itself out.

In China today Mah Jong carries overtones of pre-revolution-ary decadence, and small wonder. Here is Han Suyin's description, from 'The Crippled Tree', of her European mother's encounter with it at her first big Chinese family reunion in 1913: 'There were interminable Mah Jong parties, going on for six or seven days or nights without interruption. Twenty or thirty women collected together around the tables set up in every room, and

More Chinese ladies gambling away the hours. By courtesy of the Royal Pavilion, Brighton.

"Electrical Mah Jong". A novelty pack to cash in on a popular craze, 1930.

A modern version, made by Pentangle, Stockbridge, England, of the Chinese Nine Connected Rings puzzle. This puzzle is supposed to have been invented by Hung Ming (181—234 AD) as a pastime to keep his wife occupied while he went off to war. The Chinese name signifies "Delay guest instrument."
The wooden tangram, sometimes called the Wisdom Puzzle, is another very old Chinese puzzle. Napoleon is said to have whiled away many long hours of exile on St Helena solving its intricacies.

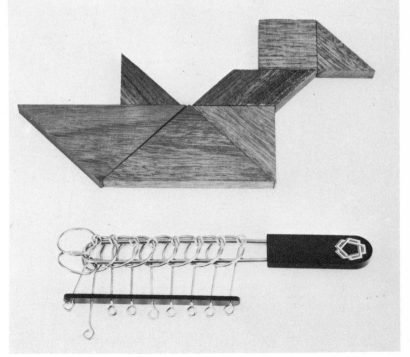

there was the eternal click and fall of the Mah Jong all the time, and the cries of the babies brought in by the Amahs—the mother not even interrupting her game while she breast-fed her child, and then handed it back to the servant. Six, seven, eight hours they played, a lunatic passion, sometimes giving their turn to someone else to go and snatch a few hours' sleep."

But whatever one may think of the social impact of the game, Mah Jong sets gave wonderful scope for Chinese craftsmanship. The 136 pieces were beautifully made, with bamboo backs decorated with ivory or bone faces, engraved and coloured, or— for very luxurious sets—composed of mother of pearl and jade. The sensuous pleasure of handling a good set was one of the charms of the game.

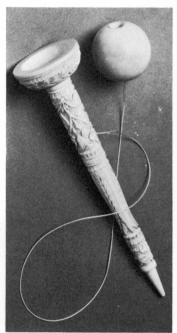

The lacquer boxes containing delicately worked ivory puzzles often contained other little toys, such as the cup and ball (above) and little carved acrobats who tumble head over heels over the bar when the knob at the side is turned.

Puzzles

A beautiful black lacquered box, decorated with trails of plum or peach blossom. On the lid, exotic little people framed in a far-away landscape of pagodas and weeping willows. Inside, each in its own meticulously lined compartment, lie ten or more intricately carved toys and puzzles: Chinese puzzles, the very symbol of oriental cunning, craftsmanship, patience and devious ingenuity.

From the late 18th century onwards these elegant boxes were exported in vast quantities to grace the drawing rooms of America and Europe. Indeed many of the puzzles, such as those in the shape of a crucifix, were expressly designed for the European market.

In the larger and more expensive boxes there could be, besides the puzzles, other intriguing little toys: a set of delicately carved spillikins; or a funny little acrobat with hinged arms and legs, who could somersault and perform erratic gymnastics hanging from a horizontal bar; and sometimes an ivory cup and ball, to be caught skilfully on the spike rather than in the cup.

The puzzles themselves usually include a tangram, fitted into its own elegant little box. The tangram is a thin square of ivory dissected into seven pieces which, by following the diagrams printed on the thin yellowy paper, you can arrange to form the outlines of countless different objects: fish, birds, animals, people —and very Western windmills, castles and houses.

Another tiny box is filled with what looks like a solid ivory cube. When you tip it out on to the table, you find it consists of ten very irregular pieces which you can try for hours on end to fit back into the box again.

In the third compartment you may find six little rods or sticks of ivory which can be locked together to form a three-dimensional cross.

A further group of puzzles consists of rings tied in various ways by silken cords to elegantly fretted pieces of ivory. One of these is known as the Chinese Ladder puzzle; another is the famous Chinese Rings puzzle, with its nine rings mysteriously attached to a loop of ivory fitted into a carved handle. This is perhaps the most characteristically 'Chinese' of all puzzles, and the oldest. There is a well-known musical drama, entitled 'The Stratagem of

An 18th century Chinese box of puzzles, made for the export market. The ladder puzzle at the side is ingeniously strung with different coloured silken cords. Each time a rung of the ladder is moved up or down, a fresh combination of colours and number of cords appears.

Interlocking Rings', which was first performed in Northern China at the beginning of the 14th century; but the origins of the puzzle are probably much earlier still: indeed, some say that the folk-hero Hung-Ming invented it 200 years before the birth of Christ. At all events it is a fiendishly difficult puzzle. The object is to remove all nine rings from the loop—an operation which involves 511 different manipulations.

One of the Chinese names for this puzzle is 'Detain your Guest'. Its complexity could be indefinitely extended by adding more loops, so that a lifetime could be wasted in trying to solve it. The principle of the puzzle can also be put to more practical uses, however, such as making efficient locks for doors and strongboxes.

The puzzle has also been discussed in some detail by mathematicians, notably by the Italian, Cardan, in the 16th century. A table published in 'Recréations Mathematiques' in Paris in 1750 explains how the various operations required to solve this puzzle can be tabulated in the form of a binary sequence.

According to M. Louis Bloncourt, who has spent many years collecting not only puzzles of all kinds but also books discussing

Illustrations from "Recreations Mathematiques", published in Paris in 1750, which examines how the Chinese Ring Puzzle can be solved, and how it can be used as an effective lock on doors or strong-boxes.

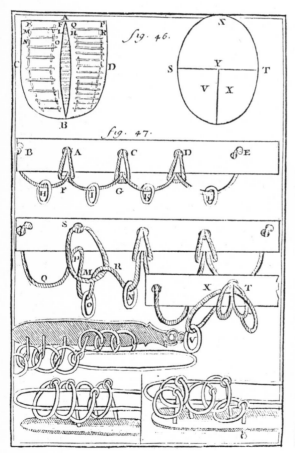

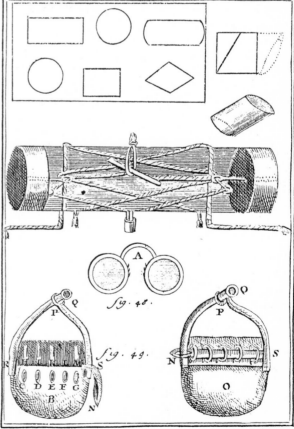

the intellectual concepts on which they are based, there are two possible ways of tackling them. Either you proceed empirically: pick the object up, and by handling it and moving the pieces hope by trial and error to hit on the solution to the problem; or you examine the puzzle carefully and work out in your mind, step by step, the actions which will have to be taken to achieve the desired end. This requires a capacity for sustained logical reasoning similar to that involved in mathematics; and it has led M. Bloncourt to advance the theory that many of these puzzles originated as exercises in concentration and part of the religious disciplines of meditation as practised in India and China.

Ivory tangram, showing how to arrange the elements of the puzzle to make these shapes.

The principles underlying these 'classical' Chinese puzzles are constantly reappearing under new names and other guises. 'The Strong Man', 'The Problem of the Sudan', and 'The Captive Heart' in the French box of puzzles 'Jeux Nouveaux Réunis' are all early 19th century versions of Chinese puzzles. Today we have similar puzzles of European provenance called 'Mao' and 'Mandarin' where plastic has replaced carved and polished ivory; and others, more elegantly fashioned in metal and wood, designed by J. C. Dalgety and produced by Pentangle. Nothing in fact has changed but the names and materials.

Chinese classical puzzles in their 19th century French disguise.

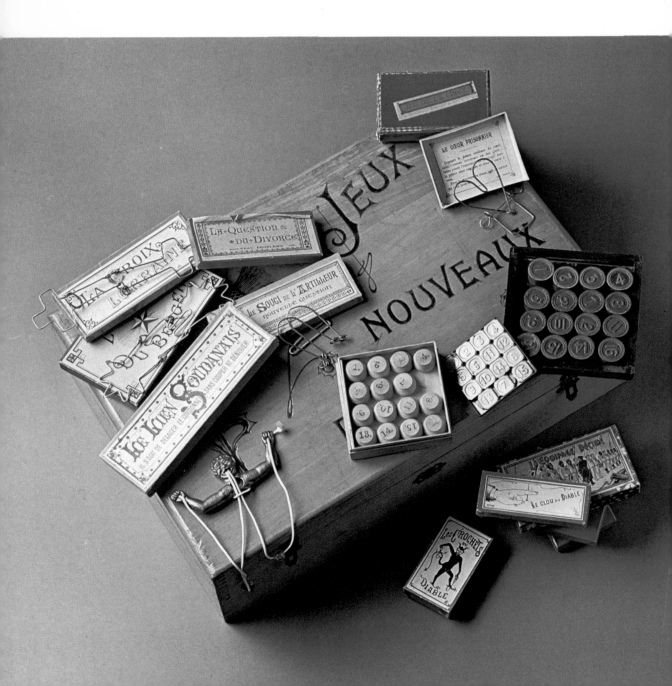

CHAPTER SIX

SWEETS AND TREATS

*Of the delight of the Chinese in
Procession, especially at weddings and
funerals. Of the Festival of Lanterns, and the
despatch of the Kitchen God to Paradise at the New
Year. Of Mooncakes and their origin, and
the Creation of the World from an Egg.*

Processions

On the rare occasions when we catch a glimpse of China on our television screens, we seem inevitably to be presented with some grand parade. There, flashing through our sitting-room, are stern young men holding aloft huge red banners, pretty young girls rhythmically waving bunches of flowers, little children flying great clouds of balloons, solemn old gentlemen advancing in stately measure beneath a forest of portraits and placards.

Processions, it would seem, have always been an enjoyable form of entertainment in China; and all the important events of one's life have traditionally been marked by some kind of public show. At births, relations and friends would arrive at the house in style, carrying duck-eggs painted red and gifts of food and clothes, and letting off strips of fire crackers. Young brides would be ceremoniously carried in red sedan chairs to their new homes, accompanied by musicians and surrounded by their dowries packed in elaborate chests. At deaths, everyone hoped the family would mark the occasion by as grand a funeral procession as finances would allow.

And just as today, if one has the money, one can call in specialist catering firms to supply a banquet or a wedding breakfast, so in earlier days China had enterprises which would hire out all the paraphernalia required to make up a procession: musicians, sedan chairs, chests, presentation gifts; mourners, coffins, catafalques, paper robes and paper effigies for burning at a funeral.

Besides these private processions, which were often marked with as much false show and ostentatious display as similar events in the West, there were all the public holidays, matching the seasons of the year. In winter, the New Year festivities, with parades of lanterns and huge papier maché dragons through the streets. In spring and early summer great family outings to tidy up family graves or watch, on the fifth day of the fifth month, the water carnivals and dragon boat races. In late summer, moonlight picnics; in autumn, kite-flying. And always there would be bright lanterns, fireworks, and special treats to eat: little blown sugar figures, coloured rice-paste moulded into fruit or flower shapes, New Year puddings, autumn mooncakes.

Lanterns

Chinese lanterns are a feature of life there which has survived the revolution: they are much in evidence at the annual October celebrations. Traditionally, however, the Festival of Lanterns was held on the 8th day of the First Moon (in February or early March).

In Part 1 of 'The Crippled Tree' Han Suyin describes how her father recalled the festival from his childhood: "Everyone went out in the evening and walked about the city streets under flower arches holding lanterns in their hands. All the shop fronts were

Top left and right: Paper lanterns.

Chinese schoolgirls performing a popular "flower" dance.

Opposite: A brightly painted dragon, moulded from incense and rice flour paste. This is burnt during religious festival days by Chinese living in Penang, Malaysia.
Below: Figures made from rice flour paste, paper and paint by itinerant street pedlars.

hung with lanterns, four or more to each shop. One year I went about carrying a huge fish with glass eyes, the paper scales so deftly knit with thin wire that they moved as I walked, and the fish swaying from side to side appeared to swim in air. Another year I had a great bird, a flying crane, the feathers of painted silk paper, each one separate—a whole plumage under my hand, warm, tender and tremulous as a live bird."

Opposite: 19th century folk print of the Kitchen God.

Chiang Yee, in his book 'A Chinese Childhood', describes how as a child he took part with his whole extended family in the Feast of Lanterns:

"In my eleventh year my family happened to have a very good year's business and a good harvest, so they decided to celebrate even more thoroughly than usual. Father and two uncles suggested that they should make a lantern show for us youngsters to manage ourselves, there being a good number in the generation. They knew that it would be very expensive and probably unsuitable to get the lanterns made by professional artists, so they set about making the whole thing themselves. One of our relations who lived in the country was invited to join in the work. Before the New Year Festival all the necessary materials were bought and after New Year's Day the work began. All the lanterns were finished by the tenth of the first month, but we were not allowed to show them until the thirteenth.

"Four of my younger girl-cousins led the show, holding four different flower lanterns. Then came three young boy-cousins, aged from five to seven, with horse lanterns. These were made in two parts, head and rear, each part being attached by a bamboo rod to a string round the waist of the boy who walked between them. Inside each part burned a candle. Five of us took part in a small dragon lantern, and one boy held a red ball lantern. Sometimes I changed places with the boy who was holding the dragon's head, for as we could not perform the dance it did not matter who held it. In the rear a young boy-cousin pulled after him a string to which was tied a large white hare lantern moving on wheels, with five little hare lanterns on top of it. They were all lit. We could not go out very far, so we displayed our lanterns in our own house for the first two nights. And then on the fifteenth

Drawings by Chiang Yee of dragon and horse lanterns.

Opposite: Carved wooden cake moulds, a mooncake, and a bamboo steamer with its tight fitting lid.

Little girl with paper windmills. These are on sale in Hong Kong during the Spring Ch'ing-ming Festival, when everyone goes out into the country to picnic and to visit the family's ancestral tombs. Here they weed and tidy up the graves, plant on them wands of paper scrolls, and burn an offering of red paper money.

Below: The Kitchen God. Folk print.

night we were invited to go to my sister's house, which was only about two hundred yards away. On our arrival the four flower lanterns moved in and out in a grand chain. Then the three horses did more or less the same. Finally, the dragon lantern made a circuit in the house and the hare lantern followed. We all enjoyed the show immensely.

"On our return, the ceremony of burning all the lanterns took place. It was the custom for all the lanterns in the Festival, whether carried by adults or children, to be burnt, indicating that the year's work began from the next day. No sooner had we finished the burning of our lanterns than our elders used to tell us to get ready for school."

Tsao Wang the Kitchen God

A picture of Tsao Wang, the kitchen god, used to hang in every Chinese kitchen and was traditionally renewed at the New Year. (This, like our Easter, was calculated from the phases of the moon, and fell between 20th January and 20th February; it was the time for paying off debts, spring-cleaning, buying stocks of

Above: To protect the main doorway of the house it was formerly the custom to paste up on either side a fierce armed warrior—one with a red face, one with a white face—to scare away any evil spirit which might try to rush in when the door was opened.

Mooncakes.

food and presents, and holding great family reunions.)

Tsao Wang was not, however, a gourmet nor an expert cook, but a kind of Father Christmas figure, skilled at assessing the goodness and badness of children. Seven days before New Year's Day he would set off for Heaven to present his annual report on the family where his picture hung. A bundle of hay and a bowl of water would be prepared for his horse, and some special sticky sweets for him to eat on the way. Then his picture would be taken down, a little honey put on his lips to sweeten his words, and the whole lot popped into the kitchen fire.

On New Year's Eve all but the very little children were allowed to stay up all night. A lamp would be lit in the kitchen to show Tsao Wang his way home. At dawn, doors and windows would all be opened, fireworks let off, incense and sweet-smelling wood burnt, and a fresh paper image of Tsao Wang pasted up on the kitchen wall. The house would also be decorated with other New Year pictures: for instance, on either side of the main gate or door two fierce-looking generals, one with a white face and the other with a black, both armed to the teeth and resplendent in old-fashioned armour. These were the guardians of the gate, put there to ward off evil spirits.

Mooncakes

Mooncakes: these are like bits of rich fruit cake baked into little moon-coloured pies. They were traditionally eaten at harvest time, when grown-ups would hold special moon-viewing parties out of doors, and children would put all their toys on show and receive presents of lanterns, new toys and mooncakes.

In the 14th century Peking housewives are said to have helped plan an uprising of Chinese nobles against their Mongol oppressors by sending out to all their friends and supporters coded messages inside their festive mooncakes.

Today fortune cookies are still made in China, in the shape of a red star containing a Thought of Chairman Mao. Those made in industrial quantities in the U.S.A. contain more mundane mottoes.

Chinese Painted Eggs and Red Duck Eggs

Mandarin Ducks are the Chinese equivalents of silver slippers, white heather, horseshoes and black cats—or other traditional emblems of luck and marriage. Eggs, painted bright red, were used to announce a 'happy event' in the family.

In many other lands also, decorated eggs are the accepted symbols of life and re-birth. In China, the story of the Creation was told to children in this way:

In the beginning

In the beginning neither Heaven nor Earth existed, only an egg-shaped Chaos. From this egg a giant was born, called

P'an-Ku. The heavy, dark yolk of the egg, the Yin, fell and
became the Earth; the light, white part, the Yang, became the Sky.
For 18,000 years the Giant became bigger and bigger, and each
day he pushed the earth and the sky further and further apart.

At last this great Giant died. His eyes became the Sun and the
Moon, his voice the roll of the Thunder; his breath the Wind and
the Storm; his bones the mountain Rocks; his flesh the fruitful
fields and the soil. Some ancient authorities say that the little fleas
which hopped about his body were transformed into human
beings.

Others say that the Giant was helped in his task of creating the
world out of Chaos by a dragon, a tortoise, and a phoenix and a
unicorn; and that before he died he made out of the elements
little man-like figures and laid them out in the sun to harden. The
first batch stayed out too long and burned black, so he put them
to live in hot countries. The second lot were only half-baked, so
these he sent to live in cold countries. But the last batch turned
out just right, a delicious, golden yellow-brown; and these
P'an-Ku placed in the fertile plains of the Middle Kingdom of
China.

Ying and Yang symbol.

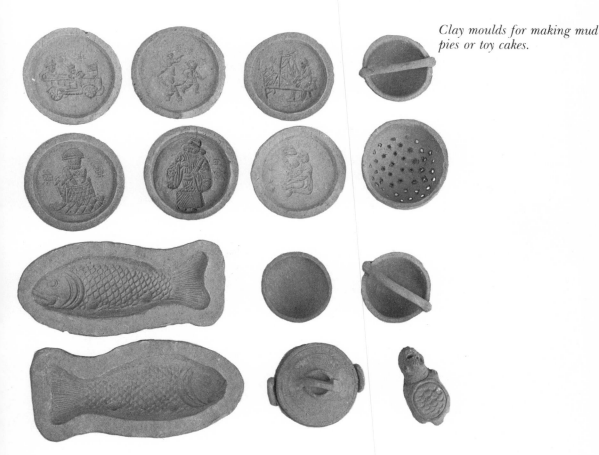

*Clay moulds for making mud
pies or toy cakes.*

Woks and Noodles

The 'wok' is an efficient, all-purpose metal cooking vessel used by every housewife in China. It has two handles and is shaped like a shallow cone.

By pouring a small amount of oil or fat in the bottom, it can be used as an economical deep-frier; or one can put water in it and use it for cooking rice, soup or noodles. And as the sides of the wok slope outwards, one can easily fix one or two latticed bamboo trays above the boiling water, put a covered lid on top and cook still more food in the steam.

The wok fits on top of a very simple cooking stove, made from a few bricks and clay. A bundle of twigs, a lump or two of coal or wood—and a meal for a large and hungry family can be cooked in a few minutes. For all Chinese cooks spend a long time preparing meat and vegetables before cooking them: everything is sliced into small, thin pieces, which heat up quickly in a little oil or water.

Knives and forks are not needed to eat these dishes, and even tiny Chinese children manage their chopsticks with remarkable ease.

Not all Chinese live on a diet of boiled rice enlivened by bamboo shoots, pickles and other tasty morsels, for rice does not grow easily in the North of China or in the mountains. In the main, however, Chinese cooks do not turn wheat and other cereal flours into loaves of bread. They save time and cooking fuel by rolling out the dough into thin sheets, cutting it into long strips and cooking it quickly in boiling water.

More windmills to welcome the Spring.

Red eggs for celebrating the birth of a child.

Cakes and biscuits.

It is said that Marco Polo bought these recipes back to his native Italy. This widespread belief is, however, contested by Signor Vincenze Agnesi, curator of the world's only Spaghetti Museum, not far from Genoa. Signor Agnesi's family have been making pasta since 1824, and among the documents displayed in his museum is a will, dated 1279, in which a Genoan soldier requests that a basket of macaroni should go to one of his heirs.

Ices

Marco Polo did not return to his homeland after his first trip to China until a few years later. But if, after all, he did not teach his fellow Italians to make spaghetti, it is still possible to believe that he brought back from China the secrets of successful ice-cream making. For according to the Larousse Gastronomique "The Chinese taught the art of making ice-cream to the Indians, the Persians and the Arabs. Ice-creams and water ices were introduced into France about the year 1660, by a Sicilian named Francisco Procopio."

Within living memory 'hokey-pokey, a penny a lump' was sold in the streets of London and other English cities by itinerant Italian ice-cream vendors.

Rhubarb, rhubarb . . .

Two hundred and fifty years ago, what Englishmen prized above tea or oranges was rhubarb, imported at great cost from China. It is said that at one time Chinese statesmen seriously considered the possibility of banning the export of rhubarb, as a means of inducing the British to be more amenable. Their reasoning was based on the theory that 'a purge of rhubarb must be physically essential to the British, with their repulsive diet of greasy meat and boiled vegetables."

A Scots doctor, John Bell, when travelling from St. Petersburg to Peking in the suite of Peter the Great's ambassador to China, dug up some rhubarb roots with his stick while taking a stroll not far from the Great Wall. He noted that where marmots had dug up the earth near their burrows great clumps of rhubarb were growing. He goes on to say:

"I have been more particular in describing the growth and management of the rhubarb, as I never met with another person who could give a satisfactory account of where and how it grows. I am persuaded that in such a dry climate as this it might be so cultivated as to produce any quantity that could be wanted."

Sixty years later another eminent Scots doctor, Sir Alexander Dick, managed to grow 9½lb per year in his Edinburgh garden and to sell it at a guinea a pound.

A traditional Chinese kitchen stove, made of baked clay. It burns wood or charcoal. On top, instead of the usual pots and pans, the special offerings to the Kitchen God have been placed. The small boy is lighting fireworks.

Chopsticks hard at work.

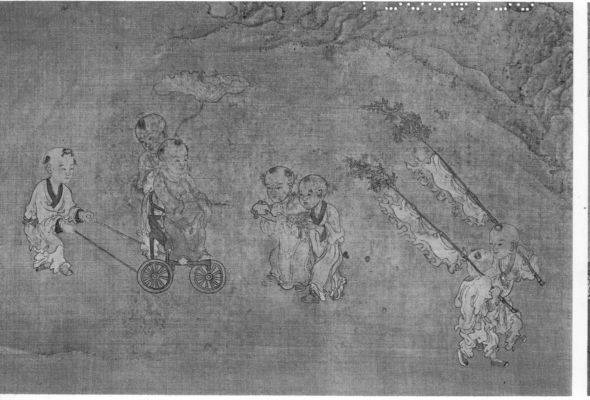

BOYS WILL BE BOYS

Rowing in a boat on a summer afternoon,
Taking baby brother for a gentle little walk,
Putting him to play in a warm, shallow bath,
Carrying your friend in a litter made of hands,
Looking for a golden toad, waving fans of palm,
Climbing up the apple tree, shooting at the birds,
Riding into battle on your faithful hobby horse,
Rolling on the ground in a horrid snarly fight—
Boys will be boys the world over.

Scenes from the Scroll of A
Hundred Sons.

Catching crickets. From an album of poems and paintings, "A Hundred Sons". The poems are by Chia Ping-Chen (1662 — 1722) and are painted on skeleton leaves from the species of tree under which Buddha was reputed to have sat. The green leaves are left to soak and rot, then gently bleached. The process was introduced into England by way of Italy during the reign of Elizabeth I, but only really became popular in the 19th century, as a Victorian ladies' pastime.

CHAPTER SEVEN
PUPPETS

Of Marionettes and other Puppets,
with divers speculations on their origins, and
examples of the folk tales which have nourished the
Chinese theatre. Of the skills of their Puppeteers,
in particular the magical effects wrought by
the manipulators of Shadow Puppets.

The Puppet Theatre

Three thousand years ago a Chinese puppet master called Yang Shih was invited to the royal palace to entertain the guests at an important state function. Everyone was enjoying the show when suddenly the emperor, in a towering rage, put a stop to the proceedings and ordered his executioners to seize the puppet master and chop off his head.

"What has caused you such displeasure, your majesty?" asked the poor man, quite bewildered.

"What indeed!" said the emperor. "Have not your actors dared to wink at the ladies of my court and to treat my guests with impertinent disrespect?"

"But, your majesty, my actors are only creatures of rag and straw," said their manipulator, and seizing a knife he slashed them open, and thereby saved his life.

Another folk tale testifies to the great antiquity of the art of puppet-making in China. During the reign of the Emperor Kao-Tzu, founder of the Han Dynasty, nomadic tribesmen (so it is said) invaded the country and laid siege to the town of Pinchen. Now the enemy were under the command of Khan Modo, well-known for his taste in pretty girls and for the extreme jealousy of his strong-willed wife. So the besieged Chinese set up on the

Rod puppets in action in an open air street booth.

Chinese mechanical figures. They were given to the British Puppet Guild in 1935, and may have come from an animated tableau in the window of a London Chinese restaurant, or from a puppet show.

Chinese peepshow.
Aquatint 1814.

Opposite: Two rod puppets.
Slender bamboo rods would be
attached to their wrists when
they were used in a
performance.

Below: A one-man glove
puppet show. Aquatint, 1799.

battlements, under the guidance of a skilful puppeteer, some beautifully dressed life-size puppets who waved and beckoned to the besiegers with all the allurements of real girls. Fearful of the power of their charms, the Khan's wife persuaded her husband to raise the siege, pack his baggage and steal away.

In his book 'The Origins of the Chinese Puppet Theatre' Sun-k'ai-ti recalls these two legends and advances the view that the puppet theatre may have been the ancestor of the classical Chinese live theatre. The stylised gait, postures and gestures adopted by live actors seem to imitate those of marionettes manipulated by strings. The unchanging designs of their facial make-up, artificial on a human face, are natural on a carved and painted wooden head. A character in classical live drama, on his first entry on stage, announces clearly who he is and what he intends to do—a very necessary convention when performing with puppets, but not essential with a human performer.

On the other hand the great Russian puppeteer, Sergei Obraztov, while unstinting in his praise of the skill of Chinese puppet masters and acknowledging that it would be gratifying to award to the puppet in China the honour of primogeniture on the stage, nevertheless thinks this improbable. "The history of the theatre," he writes, "including the puppet theatre, is as vast as the history of human society. Imitative movements addressed to audiences originally took the form of human dance-pantomines . . . . . . in which the performer was costumed in some way or other. I think that painting the face preceded the adoption of the mask. But this is not to say that later on facial make-up could not have copied the mask, or a masked human—the puppet.

"In the Chinese theatre, it seems to me easier to postulate the influence of living actors on the puppet theatre than the reverse. Yet when we find a puppet play which is identical with its counterpart on the living stage, we cannot be certain it has jumped from the footlights of the living theatre on to the puppet stage. We cannot be certain because its subject-matter did not originate in the theatre, but had its roots in literary and folk epics."

On stage the 'Monkey King' dazzles the audience with his extraordinary acrobatic dancing; and his ready wit provokes laughter whether he be a rod, a glove or a shadow puppet. All versions are stage adaptations of the picaresque novel 'Journey to the West'. The heroes and cunning Robin Hoods of the plays 'The Three Kingdoms' or 'The Men of the Marshes' perform on stage exploits which are chronicled in well-known books. Neglected heroines bewailing their fate take their cue from poems like 'The Romance of the Western Chamber'. and from fairy tales and folk legends which have been translated into every theatrical medium.

One such legend is that of Meng Chiang-Nü, the faithful wife

Paper-cut of the Great Wall of China.

whose tears caused part of the Great Wall of China to fall down.

Neil Armstrong, the American astronaut, looking down on the Earth from outer space, reported that the only man-made object they could identify was the Great Wall snaking its way from the sea to the central mountains of Asia.

The Emperor Shih Huang-ti built the Wall between the years 228 and 210 BC, rounding up countless poor labourers to slave at its construction in conditions so appalling that thousands died. According to legend, in every mile-long section a man was to be buried alive to placate the spirits of evil; but in the end only one man was thus cruelly sacrificed — a young man whose name, Wan, signified 10,000. His weeping widow, Meng Chiang-Nü, who as a baby had been found curled up inside a fairy pumpkin, set out to find him. In the words of the Peking nursery song,

The Emperor of Ch'in
Shih Huang-ti
Built a wall
From the hills to the sea.
He built it wide,
He built it stout,
To keep his subjects in

And the Tartars out.
The Emperor of Ch'in.
Meng Chiang-Nü, one sad day
From her own dear home
A thousand leagues away
To the wall did come.
Weary and worn

She wept and she cried:
"Where is my dear love
Buried inside?"
She wept and she cried
And her tears did fall,
Till down, down tumbled
That great big wall.

Traditional Chinese Nursery Rhyme

Pulling Strings

Pulling strings to make things move has been a device used with magical effect ever since prehistoric times. In the smoky recesses of their lodges and hogans American Indians could, as the medicine man sang his incantations, see before their very eyes the ears of corn grow. In ancient Egypt statues raised their arms when the gods spoke. In China the traditional skill of the puppeteer is such that every finger of the tiniest marionette seems to have a life of its own.

A Chinese street puppeteer in action. English aquatint, c. 1800.

Like the English Punch and Judy men, Chinese travelling showmen devised ingenious one-man portable booths that could be erected in a few minutes; and when the show was over everything—glove puppets, gongs, drums, playing board—could be packed up and carried away on a bamboo pole to the next street corner or market place.

The puppets we think of as essentially Chinese, however, are the intricately cut, transparent, coloured shadow figures. The equipment of a shadow puppet theatre consists of a square of white cloth stretched between four sticks of bamboo (two of them stuck upright in the ground 5 feet apart) and a bright lantern to throw the shadows on to the screen. The figures are cut out of donkey skin or parchment, tinted with translucent colours; the leaves and flowers are indicated by delicately cut tracery.

The bodies of the puppets are manipulated by rods and tiny threads. They can do amazing acrobatics and transformation tricks: a pig can turn into a camel, a fairy princess travel through the air on magic clouds. The puppets of Peking and North China are about 10—12 inches high: those of Southern China are considerably larger.

A puppet company consists of about 8 people: one or two to manipulate the puppets, two more to sing or declaim the parts and the rest to provide music on flute, drums, violin and cymbals. They would perform in tea houses, in villages, at fairs and bazaars, or at amusement centres such as the Bridge of Heaven in Peking.

Chinese shadow puppets, made of coloured translucent donkey skin. Pollock's Toy Museum. Long ago, about 100 years before the birth of Christ, an Emperor of the Han dynasty, Wu-Tei, was deeply distressed by the death of his beloved wife. The puppeteer Ciao-Meng announced that he could bring her back to life. Every night the emperor sat in his darkened room, while the spirit of his wife appeared behind a gauze screen placed in the doorway.

The 'Hundred Sons' scroll shows three boys who have rigged up a screen on a low table and are manipulating two marionettes: a gentleman scholar in a green gown and a little boy—his son perhaps. The other boys are playing the drum and beating a wooden clapper. Whether it be a stage or a puppet performance, today or in the past, all Chinese theatre is more like pantomine than anything else: there is a great deal of singing and dancing, and music comes from the same simple instruments our friends in the scroll are playing. There are round drums and oval drums, gongs, wooden clappers, a long-handled banjo, a guitar-like instrument, a flat stringed instrument and some pipes or flutes which look like a bundle of bamboo sticks stuck in a teapot. The little boy in blue running away from the phoenix at the beginning of the scroll is carrying just such an instrument; and while his bigger brothers bang away on their drums, in all probability the baby is shaking his rattle—with the same gurgling delight as the little children of Peking Man, 600,000 years ago, listened to the sounds of a pebble in a sea-shell, or the ripe seeds in a pod.

Paper-cuts of theatrical characters in military roles. The classical Chinese theatre has only four principal character types:
The acrobatic warrior, with a rich baritone voice. He always wears a long beard and gorgeous clothes, and his face is elaborately painted to *convey certain standard meanings. If red predominates, this means he is a good person; a lot of white paint indicates treacherousness; blue betokens a wild, bandit type.*
Young lovers, students and scholars are beardless, declaim in falsetto tenor voices, and are made up

The Scroll: The boys manipulate marionettes representing a gentleman scholar and his young attendant.

rather like the male actors who play female roles. The female characters can be faithful wives, virtuous daughters, acrobatic fighting girls or fast "flower" coquettes. Their make-up consists of a white cream base, pale powder and a lot of rouge on the cheeks and eyelids, while the corners of the eyes are heavily pencilled in black.

The fourth standard character, the clown, is distinguished by white patches round the eyes and nose.

PEKING NURSERY RHYME—THE ELEGANT PAGODA

How elegant is the Pagoda!
This elegant pagoda has thirteen stories.
Near the pagoda is a temple,
In the temple is an abbot,
The temple abbot has six pupils:
  Number One is Ch'ing T'ou Leng,
  Number Two is Leng T'ou Ch'ing,
  Number Three is Seng Seng Tien,
  Number Four is Tien Seng Seng,

Number Five Peng Hu Lu Pa,
  And Number Six Pa Lu Hu Peng.
Ch'ing T'ou Leng, beat the drum!
Leng T'ou Ch'ing, blow the pipe!
Seng Seng Tien, play the flute!
Tien Seng Seng, ring the bell!
Peng Hu Lu Pa, preach the sermon!
And Pa Lu Hu Peng, read the lesson!

Peking Nursery Rhyme

CHAPTER EIGHT

READING AND WRITING

壽星老兒福祿星

*Of Chinese writing materials, and
the nature and origins of the Chinese script.
Of the invention of paper by the Civil Servant
Ts'ai Lun and its dissemination, centuries later,
through Islam and into Western Europe. Of
the collecting and editing of Chinese
folk tales by the aged scholar
Pou Sing-Ling.*

Opposite: Shui Wei, a wax doll in red school uniform, made by Mrs. Margaret Glover for the Exhibition "Chinese Childhood" at Pollock's Toy Museum in 1973. A small Chinese girl visiting the Museum suggested that the doll should be called by her own name, Shui Wei, or "Emily" if that was easier.

Reading and Writing

The children in the scroll are now sitting quietly on a mat reading and writing. Their writing materials are spread around: long lengths of soft white paper, that are rolled up when finished like the scroll we have been looking at; brushes of bamboo, with tips made of several layers of different kinds of hair to meet different needs: the hair of weasels, sheep, horses, badgers, squirrels, dogs, deer, musk-rats and many other animals.

The ink for painting or for writing is made by pouring a little water on a stone and rubbing into it a tablet of hard, black ink. The tablet is made from glue, with a drop of perfume, mixed with the soot collected from rows of tiny lamps burning sesame or rape seed oil.

To read even the simplest story, Chinese children have to work very hard and to learn to recognise a thousand or more little picture signs. But once he has accomplished this basic task, a reader of Chinese today could manage to make out what was written by the remote ancestors of living Chinese people three thousand years ago.

The Scroll: The boys are sitting on a rug, reading and writing.

In 1899, at Chang-te-fu in Honan Province, a deposit of

An oracle bone dating from 1400—1100 BC. British Museum.

Wooden strip used for record keeping in 100 AD. British Museum.

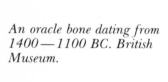
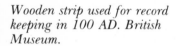

thousands of fragments of bones and tortoise shells was unearthed; and when the bones were cleaned it was seen that they were engraved with the earliest known form of Chinese writing.

The bones date from about 1500 BC, and the inscriptions are all questions concerning the future: "Will the harvest be a good one?" "Will the rain fall?" "If we go hunting tomorrow, shall we capture any game?" Sometimes the answers are written on the same shell.

In ancient China tortoises were regarded as sacred animals; and perhaps as they live so long and look so venerable and wise, it was thought that they had foreknowledge of the future, and therefore their carapaces were used in fortune-telling.

In other parts of Central Asia divination was practised by observing the shoulder-blade of a sheep when it had been scorched over a fire. From the resulting cracks in the bone the future was predicted—just as people do today when they read the tea leaves in a cup; and from these same cracks Chinese pictogram writing gradually evolved. On ancient bowls and weapons we can see how these pictograms became more and more stylised. Emperors used tablets of jade for writing on, grand nobles and high officials tablets of ivory.

Later on a pointed bamboo stick, dipped in black varnish made from the sap of the lacquer tree, was used for writing short messages on wooden boards. If the message was over 100 words, it was written out on slips of bamboo; these narrow bamboo tablets were then piled up into a pack and joined together by a thin leather strap or a silk cord, which was passed through holes pierced at the top of each slip. This explains why Chinese is still written vertically down the page and why Chinese books start on what seems to Europeans to be the back page.

The earliest printed text in the world, dated 11 May 869 AD. It is part of the Diamond Sutra, a prayer to Buddha to be repeated over and over again. The text would have been carved on one block of wood, the illustrations on another. British Museum.

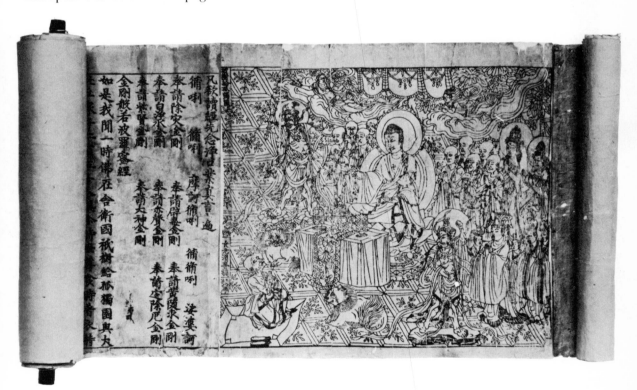

Ts'ai Lun and the Invention of Paper

The invention of paper is a landmark in the intellectual development of mankind.

The man to whom we are indebted for this far-reaching discovery was named Ts'ai Lun. He was born in Southern China and became an important civil servant, then Director of the Imperial Arsenals. He was of an enquiring mind, and spent all his

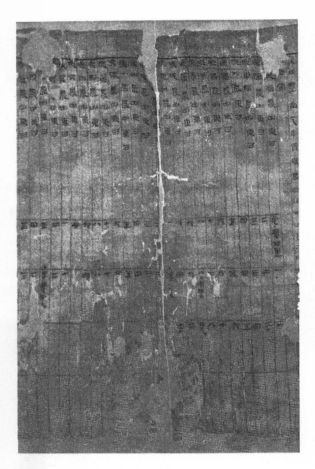

Books copied on to silk. From a recently excavated tomb near Chungsa in Hunan. They date from c. 200 years BC.

spare time in study. This is how his great invention is chronicled in the annals of the later Han dynasty:

"From times of old, documents had been written on bamboo boards fastened together. There was also paper made of silk refuse. But silk was too expensive, and the bamboo boards were too heavy: both were inconvenient. Therefore Ts'ai Lun conceived the idea of using tree bark, or bast fibre, hemp, and also old rags and fishing nets, for making paper. In 105 AD he submitted his invention to the Emperor, who lauded his skill. From this moment there was no one who did not use his paper, and throughout the Empire all people called it the paper of the Honorable Ts'ai."

Ts'ai Lun lived for another thirteen years after his great invention. Intrigues at court then drove him to despair, and he committed suicide by swallowing poison. It is said that he first manufactured paper from fishing nets by the side of a pool near the town of Tsao-yang in Hupeh Province; and his art is hereditary among the people of that district.

The manufacture of paper remained a Chinese monopoly until the year 751, when some Chinese prisoners of war were brought to Samarkand. Some of them were paper-makers, and their secrets and skills were used to set up a paper mill there. In 794 the Calif of Baghdad, Harun-al-Raschid, set up manufactories of his own, and

Carved seals. An early form of printing.

The Scroll: One of the five scholarly comments which follow the paintings on the Scroll of A Hundred Sons.

from Persia the industry spread to all Islamic countries—Arabia, Syria, Egypt, Spain. In 1150 a paper-mill was founded at Fabriano in Italy, and from Italy the art was acquired in France and Germany.

The Revocation of the Edict of Nantes in 1699 brought many French paper-makers into exile in England. These workmen could not however print 'pagoda-papers', which were imported by Dutch merchants from China and sold at exorbitant prices to those who wished to be fashionable. 'Pagoda-papers' were colour-printed 12 inch squares of wallpaper: they had been used for centuries by the Chinese to decorate the walls and ceilings of their rooms.

A page from an illustrated children's reader first published in 1436. Perhaps the oldest illustrated reader in the world, it has 306 drawings and illustrates 388 Chinese characters.

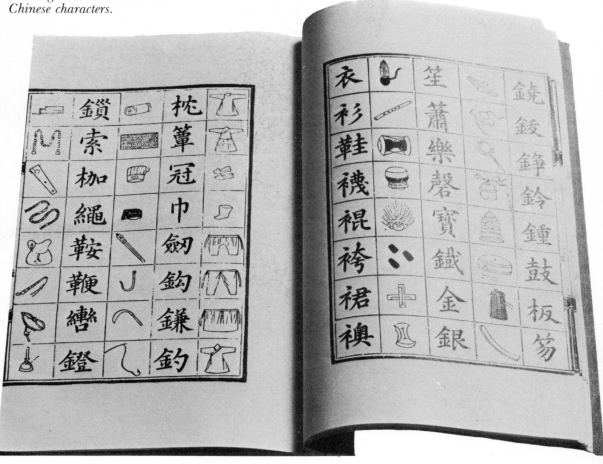

In recent times there has been an ever-increasing demand for paper. Millions of people have been taught to read the new, simplified form of Chinese writings: millions of inexpensive textbooks have been published for schools, as well as other children's books; and the circulation and readership of newspapers is constantly increasing. With a skill and ingenuity comparable to Ts'ai Lun's, Chinese paper manufacturers are using many different raw materials to make the cellulose pulp: straw, grass, rice and sugar-cane stalks, and all kinds of reeds growing in ponds and swampy land along the edges of the rivers.

The Library of Strange Events

Some time near the year 1715 a very old scholar sat writing at his desk late one night.

"With only an autumn glow-worm to light me," he wrote, "I struggle against the will-o'-the-wisps of old age. Like a speck of dust in a beam of sunlight, I am nothing more than a comic joke for

A modern reading book, published in Hong Kong.

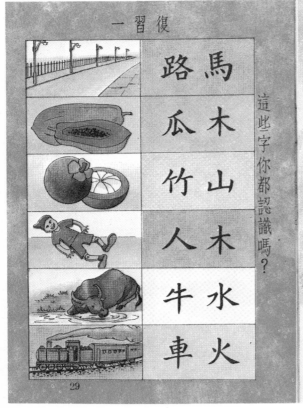

today's wits. I ask my friends to jot down any old tales they remember and I struggle to shape them into a story. Midnight finds me brush in hand; the lamp burns low; outside, the melancholy wind blows. Stooping over my simple work table I struggle on, slowly piecing my fables together, bit by bit."

Shortly afterwards he died, at the great age of 93. His name was Pou Sing-ling. He died poor, unrecognised, unknown, having spent the last thirty-six years of his life gathering together, editing, transcribing, and giving literary form to the greatest collection ever of Chinese folk tales, *"The Library of Strange Events"*, as he called his work. In 1740 his grandson managed to get the manuscript published, and from that time on Pou Sing-ling's stories have been read and re-read by generations of Chinese children.

Here is one concerning a young scholar named Chou, who was living humbly in the Capital City. One day Chou went with a friend out into the country to visit a small monastery. An old ragged priest showed them around. There was nothing much to see except a beautifully carved Buddha, seated in a little chapel whose walls

Children's Health Service in China today.

were painted with pictures of animals, gods and goddesses. One of these celestial girls was picking flowers: a gentle smile hovered over her lips; her long black hair hung down in two braided plaits. Chou noticed her, and gazed at the picture in unblinking admiration. Suddenly he felt himself floating in the air, as if riding on a cloud. Then he was on the other side of the wall, and the houses stretched out far from each other, unlike those in the mortal world.

A large crowd had gathered to listen to a priest preaching the word of Buddha. Chou joined them, then felt someone plucking at his sleeve. He turned round, and there was the girl in the painting he had admired. Smiling at him, she led the way to a charming little house, and motioned Chou to enter.

Chou went in and knelt down before her. A group of girls then arrived carrying gifts of ribbons, hairpins and other pretty ornaments.

"Dear friend," they declared, "now that you are married you must put your hair up." They combed out the plaits, amid much laughter, and did the girl's hair up in the style of a married woman.

Schoolgirls dressing up.

Chou's bride looked still more charming, and he was just about to embrace her tenderly when there arose outside the sound of angry voices and the clink of arms.

Chou jumped to his feet and cautiously peeped through the lattice window. Outside stood a giant in golden armour, chains and whips in his hands.

"Some mortal has made his way in here. I must search him out," he roared.

"Quick, quick," said the startled nymph. "Hide under the bed. Don't breathe! Don't move!" Quickly she slipped out to join her friends. Chou heard a great stamping of heavy boots as people came in and out of the room. Then the hue and cry faded away into the distance. Chou remained hidden under the bed, still petrified.

Meanwhile, back in the chapel, Chou's friend began to worry about his absence. "Where can he have gone?" he asked.

"Oh, he is not far away," replied the priest; and tapping gently on the wall he whispered "Chou, your friend is waiting for you. He is growing impatient."

Suddenly Chou's outline appeared on the wall, and a split second later he was standing in the middle of the room, rigid as a block of wood, his eyes staring. Then he started to tremble.

"Whatever happened to you?" asked his friend.

"I heard a noise like a great clap of thunder," said Chou, and he turned and looked once more at the painting on the wall. The girl

Opposite: A science lesson.

Below: A school outing.

in the picture had her long, hanging plaits bound up in the style of a married woman.

"What can this mean?" Chou and his friend exclaimed.

"Visions come to those who see them," replied the old priest, as he shambled off.

Visiting Peking.

Left: No sex discrimination today in China.

Below: From Hong Kong: picture cards for learning to read

The French magazine Elle, famous for its smart dress sense, its cookery recipes and its sharp, practical answers to readers' letters, added yet another useful column to its pages: elementary Chinese lessons, showing how basic words derived from pictograms and in what order the different strokes of the pen should be made.

Cliff

Rocks

Father (the whip hand)

Child

Mother

Raindrops.

CHAPTER NINE

THREADING NEEDLES BY MOONLIGHT

*In which are described the binding
of Chinese girls' feet; the Chinese extended
family, and the roles of its female members; the
restricted lives of Chinese girls in the past;
and the delicate charm of their embroideries
and of the stories they told as they
threaded their needles.*

Opposite: Embroidery frame, silkworm cocoons in a basket, Chinese scissors and a thimble. Chinese thimbles are narrow metal bands, worn between the first and second joints of the middle finger. The movement of the needle is away from the body, not towards it as in Europe. From Han times until quite recently needles were very short, and slightly conical in shape; and the eye was not flattened as in modern needles.

Below: Mrs Virgo's wax doll, with part of her Chinese trousseau. She has three complete outfits, consisting of trousers, pleated overshirts, tunics, headbands and shoes.

Seventy years ago, in Peking, the Chinese nanny of a little English girl made for a strange wax doll a wardrobe of exquisitely sewn Chinese clothes. There are embroidered headbands, pleated satin skirts, cross-over tunics, tiny slippers.

From its wrinkled brown face the beady, blue eyes of the doll stare up enigmatically. Is this a European expatriate re-dressed 'à la chinoise'? Mrs. Virgo, the doll's owner, can only remember her devoted amah making the clothes.

The doll's feet are perhaps a vital clue. Modelled in wax, they are of normal shape and size. Surely, if this doll had been 'made in China' to represent a genteel Chinese lady, its feet would be minute bandaged stumps? Just so, it could be argued, but Manchu gentlewomen and other classes of women in China did not bind their feet. In all probability the Chinese amah herself, like all household servants, had not had her feet bandaged and deformed in childhood.

"What strange things women will do in the name of fashion!" comments the French missionary Father Huc in 1840. "In Europe waists are tightly constricted in whalebone cages, and here in China for the past thousand years tiny, deformed feet have been à

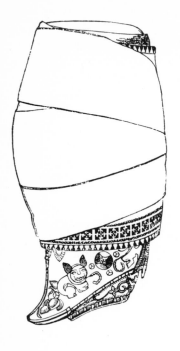

la mode. However," observes this astute French priest, "Chinese women do not find it quite so difficult to walk as one might think. When one sees them tottering along the street on their goat feet, one fears that at any moment they will stumble and fall; yet more often than not this fragile, swaying gait is put on for show. For when they think no one is watching they can run, jump and play about with remarkable ease. The favourite game of young Chinese girls is a form of battledore, but instead of having racquets they catch the shuttlecock on the heels of their little slippers."

A few years later an English missionary, Rev. Justus Doolittle, writing about the social life of the Chinese, explains how and why Chinese mothers cripple their little daughters. They do not, like Cinderella's sisters, chop off their heels or toes, but bandage the children's feet so tightly that they are compelled ever afterwards to walk on the stumps of their toes, so that even when they are fully grown they can jam their feet into shoes not more than 3 inches long. "This," adds Rev. Doolittle, "is done solely as a mark of status, of class distinction. Small feet are not an index of wealth, but of gentility. Manchu-Tartars do not allow their women to bind or cramp their feet: it unfits a beauty for entrance into the imperial harem. But many poor Chinese families struggle along,

Tiny embroidered shoe on a traditionally deformed Chinese foot.

Shaving the baby's head. All the little boys in the Scroll of A Hundred Sons have their heads shaved. This was done to both boys and girls from the age of one month till about 6 or 7 years. Only a few tufts were left, sometimes plaited and tied with a coloured ribbon. The object was to make their hair grow thick and strong: it explains the many nursery rhymes which start "This little baldhead . . ." — a Chinese term of endearment to a little baby, not to some kind old gentleman.

"The Baby's Mother"—an illustration from Child Life in China, by Mrs Bryson of the London Mission in Tientsin, published in 1900.

bringing up their daughters with small feet, rather than allow them to grow large and enable the girls to carry burdens, and do heavy work. Daughters with small feet can hope to marry into more respectable and literary families."

What a mysterious business its is, catching the attention of Prince Charming! Kind African mothers hung great weights on the ear lobes of their little daughters, or extended their lips with huge wooden discs. Grand Duchesses at the court of Louis XV saw to it that their girls were taught to glide about in huge panniered dresses, balancing immense wigs of powdered horsehair on their heads. Devoted Victorian mammas perservered with deportment chairs, backboards and tightly-laced stays. And we still read with interest of Cinderella's ordeal, dancing until midnight in hard glass slippers. Purists will comment that in China they were gold shoes, and that in M. Perrault's version they were made of 'Vair'; but to wear the incongruous with your party dress, whether it be fur-lined boots or bedroom slippers, is still a nightmare ordeal to dream about.

Overleaf: A Summer's Day a Thousand Years Ago. Painting on silk, Sung Dynasty, c. 78—805 AD. Metropolitan Museum of Art, New York (Fletcher Fund).

Opposite: Today, vinyl and plastic dolls are made not for export only, but for Chinese children to play with. This little girl in her Nursery School will have a totally different upbringing from her grandmother's. She will learn to read and write. When she grows up she can become an engineer, a doctor, a teacher, even a soldier — just like her brother. But if her skill lies in her nimble fingers, she can still earn her living creating delicate silk embroideries.

Little girls sewing. Modern paper-cut.

And in criticising foot-binding and the way many girls were brought up in China Father Huc and Rev. Doolittle were only echoing the bitter comments of the Chinese poet who wrote:

"When a son is born, he sleeps in a bed, plays with pearls and is dressed in fine robes: he is a prince who has everyone at his beck and call. But when a girl is born, she is put on the ground with only a thin coverlet, her only toy a bit of broken tile. She is good for nothing, except to prepare food and wine and not cause her parents any trouble."

The painted scroll we have been unrolling only depicts little boys, and indeed is called 'A Hundred Sons': for in the past, in China as in many other mainly agricultural societies, boys were welcome additions to the family man-power, whereas girls were not so useful. They had to be fed, protected, looked after; then, when they were old enough, married off into some other family, taking their dowry with them. So their education was restricted to what was considered useful: they did not go to school to learn to read and write: they were taught how to cook, preserve, pickle with great skill practically every edible thing. If they were intelligent and had the necessary force of character they could hope, by the time they reached old age, to be managing the economy of a very large household indeed. For in those days it was usual for families to keep together: uncles, aunts, sisters, cousins all living in separate rooms round a central courtyard, but eating in a communal dining-room, meeting in the ancestral hall to discuss family matters. They might employ a few servants, or occasionally call in outside help to do a job they could not tackle themselves. But mainly they were

self-sufficient: one relation would take care of the home doctoring, growing all the necessary medicinal herbs; another see to the accounts; another set up school to teach the boys to read and write. And of course all the clothes would be made, washed and mended at home, and sewing became the main occupation of little girls in such families. As they grew older, making their wedding trousseaux and stocking their bottom drawers absorbed all their creative instincts.

Opposite: Boy's embroidered clothes, late 19th century. In summer, Chinese children used to wear silken, pyjama-like outfits (then, as now, small boys' pants were conveniently slit at the back). In winter, they would wear layers of quilted and padded silk or cotton jackets.

Below: Baby's slippers, embroidered with tiger faces to ward off evil spirits.

There were tunics and sleeve bands to embroider; designs of mandarin ducks, butterflies, lotus flowers and plum blossom to be created, then sewn on to bed curtains, quilts and pillow-cases; purses and little cases to be decorated as presents to all members of the family; slippers to be embroidered with tigers' faces for little brothers and sisters; and finally, when they were safely married, little patchwork coatees to be made for their new-born babies out of scraps of silk provided by friends and relatives—a 'hundred families' coat', destined to cloak the little infant with the love and good wishes of all the family friends.

Raising silkworms, making, weaving silk, and embellishing it with beautiful and elaborate embroidery have played such a large part in Chinese women's lives that many proverbs and stories naturally reflect these concerns. "It is easier to thread needles by moonlight than to hold a thread straight when the wind blows" is an old Chinese saying.

Black paper-cuts in the traditional Northern style.

Paper cuts

The paper patterns used for repeat designs in embroidery work have, over the past 30 years or so, formed the basis of a popular new art form in China.

When undertaking a large-scale embroidery, it was usual to sketch out the design directly on to the length of silk to be worked. If however flowers, phoenixes or other conventional motifs were going to be repeated several times, the motif could be cut out in thin paper, then pinned to the material and covered with embroidery stitches. Several layers of paper could be cut out freehand with ordinary sewing scissors. Some women were so skilful at this that they were able to earn a living by sales of their work: for this type of cottage industry thicker piles of paper would be cut out, with sharp, chisel-like knives, punches and gouges.

These paper patterns were so cheap and so pretty that when the time came to spring-clean, decorate and prepare for the New Year, many women would cut out these motifs in slightly thicker red or black paper and stick them on to the translucent white paper which covered the unglazed window-openings of their houses.

In 1940 the Lu Hsun Art Academy in Yenan hailed these embroidery patterns, as well as the stencils used for decorating lacquer ware, as a "truly national folk art." Since then books,

research, exhibitions and competitions have helped to extend the size and range of subjects treated.

Today it is possible to distinguish separate schools and techniques. First there are the traditional red and black paper cut-outs which come from Shansi and other Northern provinces: as they were originally intended to be seen as window silhouettes, they are bold and simple.

Then, there are the theatrical cut-outs. In 1897, near Wei in the Northern province of Hopei, a small boy aged 7 called Wang Lao-shan was taken to see a performance of the Peking Opera. He was entranced, and longed to see the fantastic heroes and heroines

sing and declaim once again. He knew that shadow puppets were made from very thin pieces of donkey-skin, cut out, painted and varnished: could he not do the same thing using just paper, with the scissors from his mother's work basket? He set to work, painting the paper and cutting carefully; and by the time he was 12 years old his paper cut-out figures were known and admired by everyone in his village.

As Wang grew older he had of course to work on the farm; but when the autumn harvests were all gathered in he could devote longer hours to his favourite pastime. His skill and reputation increased over the years; and by the time he was an old man his paper-cuts of theatrical characters had set the style for all the work produced in the surrounding district.

Nanking, Soochow, Changsu and Hanchow in the maritime provinces of Kiangsu and Chekiang have been since ancient times renowned for their beautiful brocades, fine silks and elaborate motifs of their embroidery, especially flowers and fruits, often framed in a border of intricate geometrical designs.

For the Spring festivities, the emperors of the T'ang dynasty presented to the court and to their guests silken pennants deco-

Opposite: Paper-cuts embellished with gold foil. From Southern China.

Folded paper butterfly.

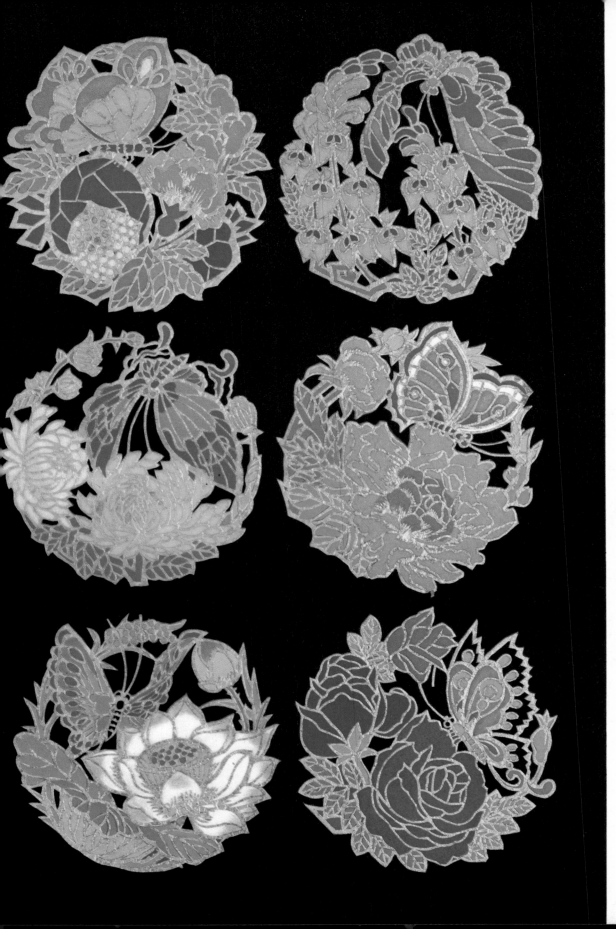

rated with words of greeting cut out in letters of gold or silver foil and in Southern China today, in and around the town of Foshan in Kwantung Province, the same technique is still in use. Tissue-thin copper foil is cut out and stuck on sheets of glossy, coloured paper; then sometimes further embellished by overpainting parts of the design in water colour.

Schoolboy designing paper-cuts.

*Embroidery pattern paper-cuts
from Shanghai.*

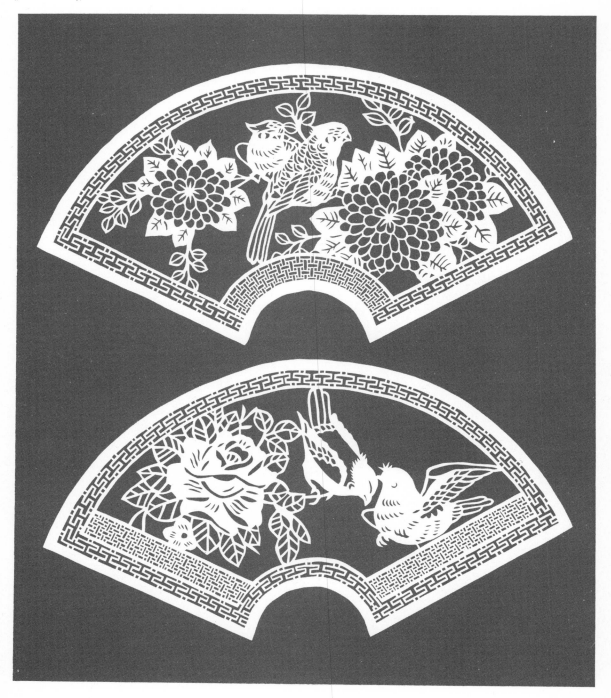

The Herd boy and the Spinning maid

Glove puppets wearing elaborate embroidered dresses.

A favourite Chinese fairy tale relates how once upon a time, long ago, the Empress of the Chinese Heavenly Kingdom had a beautiful Spinning Maid, who sat at her loom making gossamer-fine silk cloth for the gods. But the maid fell in love with a handsome young cowherd and neglected her work. This made the Empress so angry that she changed them into two bright stars, and with her silver hair-pin she drew between them a line of stars right across the sky. This River of Stars flowed down to earth, its shining

19th century embroidered purses.

silver becoming a muddy yellow as it poured through the land of China.

The Spinning Maid wept so bitterly that the Emperor of Heaven took pity on the unhappy lovers and decreed that once a year, on the seventh day of the seventh month, they could meet each other for a brief reunion.

On this day Chinese girls would hunt around the courtyards of their houses looking for a perfect spider's web to bring them luck with their embroidery. At midday they would put bowls of water in the sun and float tiny needles on the surface, in order to tell their fortunes by the shapes of the shadows cast by the needles. Later on they would hold needle-threading contests by moonlight.

Rag doll made by Ada Lunn. Ada Lunn ran an antique shop in Nanking Road, Shanghai. She designed these dolls in 1920 for sale to the Europeans who then lived in China. After 1949 Ada Lunn moved her workshop to Hong Kong, where she continued to make dolls. The stuffed rag dolls produced today by the Welfare Handicrafts and other Christian missionary organisations in Hong Kong are very similar in design to the original Ada Lunn dolls.

The Princess and The Horse

Once upon a time, long, long ago, a Chinese Emperor was out riding when robbers, springing out of a thicket, dragged him to the ground. The horse escaped, and galloped back to the palace yard.

"Whatever has happened to my husband?" said his wife, the Empress, and she sent out the palace guards to find him.

Night came, and the search parties returned without a single clue. At dawn next day the Empress, worried and tired after a sleepless night, declared "If anyone can find my husband, he can marry my youngest daughter."

The horse pricked his ears, neighed loudly, and set off in a wild gallop through the fields, returning late at night with his master on his back. The congratulations and the rejoicings were however disturbed by the unprecedented racket created by the horse, who stamped his hoofs, neighed incessantly, and banged around in his stall all night long.

In the morning, as the stable lads tried to calm the horse, the Empress, quite exasperated, said "All right, all right, but a promise made to a man cannot be claimed by a horse." Whereupon the

Opposite: Scoubidou. In 1960 French children discovered a new pastime: plaiting together different coloured plastic strands. It was a modern version of the ancient craft of plaiting "Corn Dollies". Plastic coated wire for electric circuits provided excellent material within reach of all; and as the craze spread, a number of schools, stripped of their wiring for lighting and heating, had to be closed. In China, schoolgirls plait away with the same dexterity as little French girls and, no doubt, a less imperialistic view of the possible sources of raw material.

Below: Stuffed rag tigers.

horse's anger seemed to redouble, and by evening everyone's nerves were on edge, frayed by the incessant noise. The Emperor, thinking the horse seriously distempered, took his great bow and shot an arrow through its heart. The horse was then flayed and its skin pinned to dry on to a large tree trunk.

Next day, as the Emperor's youngest daughter was passing by the tree, the horse's skin rose up and whipped itself so tightly round the girl that she was strangled, and died immediately.

In deepest mourning, the grief-stricken parents buried their daughter, still tightly enshrouded in the horse's skin, at the foot of the tree. The following year, in the spring, one of the palace servants noticed that the leaves of the tree were being devoured by white grubs with vaguely horse-shaped heads. When all the young leaves had been devoured, the insects wound themselves up in a tight cacoon of gossamer-like threads.

Seeing this, the Emperor instructed her serving maids to unwind the threads and weave them into a thin, soft, beautiful material: the first silk produced by human hands. This is why it was customary in China long ago, in April when the mulberry leaves began to unfurl, to burn a few sticks of incense before the guardian of the silkworms, represented by a statuette of a young girl dressed in flowing robes, with a horse's skin draped round her shoulders.

*In 1919 a medical missionary
in China brought this little
Door of Hope doll back to his
niece Norah. She called him
her little Chinese husband
Chang, and loved him dearly.
They had a very large family
of 13 children.
Over half a century later,
when Chang was given to
Pollock's Toy Museum, Norah
(Mrs de Courcy) could still
remember their names: Phyllis,
Chimpie, Gertie, Willie, Jane,
Eddie, Algernon, Cyril,
Darling, Cocky Olly Bird,
Miss Wobbler and Polly Wolly
Doodle. Some of them have
survived to this day.*

*Chinese Doll made in the
Door of Hope Mission. This
was a Protestant Evangelical
Missionary Home founded in
1901 in Shanghai by Miss
E. Abercrombie, to rescue
Chinese girls who had been
kidnapped or sold into slavery:
it was disbanded in 1951.
The girls did fine embroidery
and dressed dolls which were
sold in the European
concession.*

CHAPTER TEN

BUILDING FOR A NEW WORLD

*In which is surveyed the industry
of toy-making in China today; its nature
organisation and exporting procedures; and
some popular pastimes of children, such as
collecting stamps and badges. And in
which children living in Central
Europe describe their
imported Chinese toys.*

"Then all the family, Mama, Papa, my two sisters, my brothers and I went to the toyshop, and each of us chose the toy we liked best" could be the caption of this gay little painting by a Chinese child.

Aeroplanes, tip-up lorries, mechanical excavators, plastic ducks, rubber balls fill the shelves of this Chinese emporium: toys just like those that today fill the dreams of children throughout the world. Indeed, in many cases they are the same toys.

Attila Kelemen, who lives in Budapest, sent his Satellite Mystery Action for inclusion in this book, with the following letter:

"Now I have three Chinese toys. One of them is a grabber, which is for road-building—even I can grab some earth or sand with it. One has to press a handle and then the mouth of the grabber opens. This toy does not contain any motor; it rather resembles a flier-car.

"Then, I have a tank which works with a battery. It can advance and reverse and it shines at the same time. The only problem is that its batteries run down very quickly.

"The third one is a pencil-sharpener, having a tortoise shell with a mobile head.

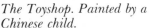

The Toyshop. Painted by a Chinese child.

"*Daddy has told me that Hungary buys from the People's Republic of China to the value of 14-15 million forints, but pays for it in Swiss francs. 98% of the toys are made of metal: ambulance car, fire engine, tourist's bus, tractor, etc. A helicopter with red cross, running with flier, can also be seen in the shop windows. There are windable toys with springs, too, e.g. a teddy-bear that is turning round and making foto with a flash.*

"*There is another interesting—rarely available—toy resembling a satellite. Its name is Satellite Mystery Action and it works with magnetism.*"

The Chinese Satellite Mystery Action.

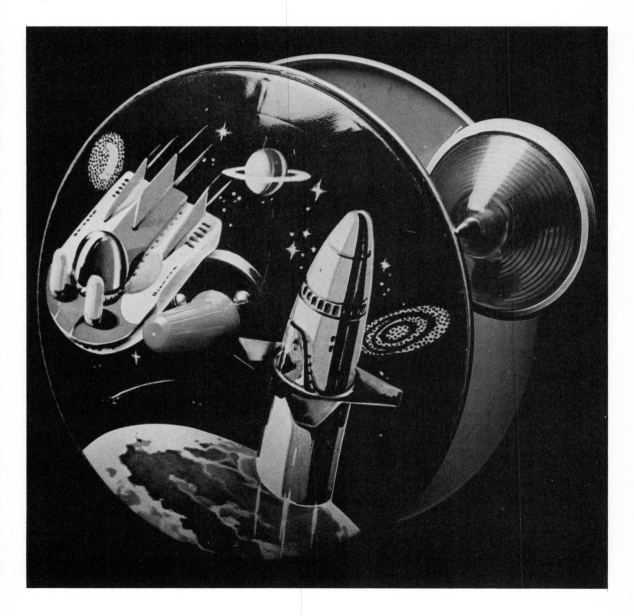

On the shores of Lake Balaton: Attila Kelemen with his Chinese "Road Building Grabber."

Chinese fluffy rabbits.

Danko Jevtovič of Belgrade, who is a year older than Attila, undertook to make a survey of toys marked 'Made in China' to be found in Belgrade shops. Here is his report:

"Beograd, 29.2.76.

1. Duck pushing cart. The duck has a cook's cap on the head. A sunshade is on the cart for selling ice-cream.

2. Blow-out dragon. A tube made out of paper, bent as a snail. When you blow, then you can hear a whistle and the tube with a feather on its end straightens itself.

3. A car made out of metal, about 15cm long, with an open roof and two men sitting inside. To move it, you have to push it and then you can hear some knocking.

4. A lorry made out of metal, about 20cm long, with an elevator and hook. This you can move with a little handle. The lorry moves itself by pushing.

5. A car made out of metal, about 15cm long. It is possible to lift the roof by a handle, and then you get a cabriolette.

6. A lorry about 10cm long with only 3 wheels. It has a large space for load. To move it, you have to push it.

7. A locomotive—without train and rails. When you push it, it moves and a lid opens itself on the roof; the head of the driver gets up and down through the hole; at the same time through the chimney you can see sparks (from a flintstone).

8. An open sports car with the driver sitting inside. There is a multicoloured wheel on the front of it, which rotates when you push and move the car."

"We have plenty of oil"—a co-operative effort by three eight year old boys.

In English shops, many of the stuffed toys, fluffy animals, plastic pencil sharpeners and fireworks on sale have been imported from China—either direct, or through Hong Kong. In 1966, one large British firm alone was importing £¼ million worth of toys every year. Since 1967, however, in Great Britain as in other EEC countries very stringent regulations about toy safety have gradually become law. In consequence, there has been some falling off of imports from China, as certain metal and painted toys did not conform with the very exacting standards imposed in Western Europe.

How and where are toys made in China today? Mr. Bernard Buckman, an English businessman who knows the China market well, explains:

"Toys are made in small factories, in small and medium workshops, in houses, in schools, Technical Institutes, Children's Cultural Centres. Sometimes a part of a toy is made in a workshop or factory and it is finished in somebody's home. Women's groups paint and trim a lot of toys.

"The selection is influenced by children, by women, by teachers, by books both domestic and foreign, and by customers from Japan,

A difficult decision in a Hong Kong toyshop.

Hong Kong, Singapore, Macao and so on. The customer brings a sample and says 'Quote me for 10,000 or whatever of this and that'.

"Dolls are another matter, since they make so many different types—from Old Peking and Canton Opera models, to provincial and minority races types, to workers in every kind of job on land, sea and air.

A tin, battery operated ping-pong match, bought in Peking.

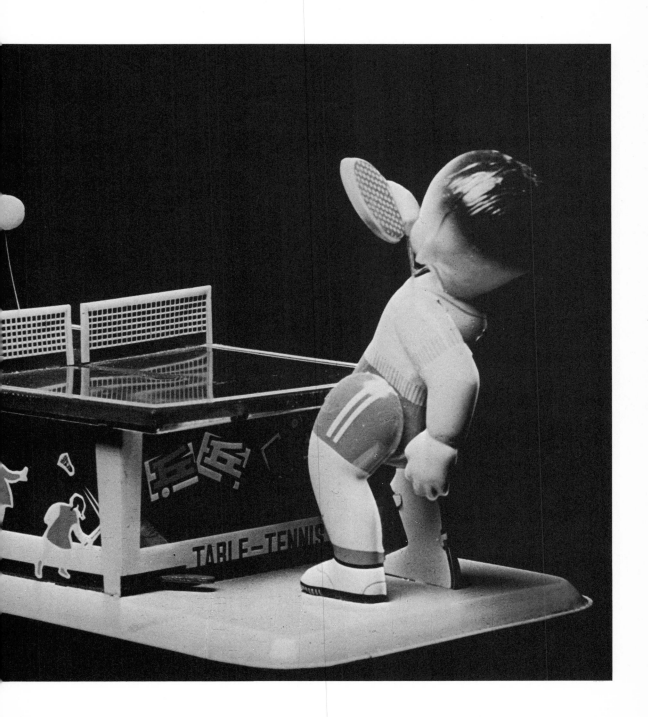

*Opposite: A few years ago
many boys were making
collections of Chairman Mao
badges.*

Below: Peking toyshop.

"During the Cultural Revolution many toys reflected current political thinking. Similarly, during the period of political bitterness between the U.S.A. and China, many toys depicted warlike pursuits—as Western toys never cease to do.

"All toys are distributed by the China National Light Industry Corporation, Peking. They have branches in Shanghai, Tientsin, Kwangchow and Swahow."

Wooden construction blocks which form pictures of oilwells; plastic dollies and mechanical toys; children's paintings which show us red fire engines, cars, lorries and bicycles dashing along city streets or railway engines and factory chimneys smoking away in the countryside—this is a very different world from that of the traditional Chinese picture of ricefields, willow trees and water buffaloes. The quiet, secluded garden where the children on the Scroll of 'A Hundred Sons' played their gentle games is indeed

Opposite: Wooden construction sets and building blocks.

Below: Toys bought in Peking in 1971. The plastic push-button soldier is bayonetting a kneeling GI. The other soldier doll has the Little Red Book, the Thoughts of Chairman Mao, in his breast pocket.

centuries away; yet the toys which feed the imagination of today's children are still, in the main, manufactured in conditions which recall the cottage industries of the Industrial Revolution rather than the giant complexes which have replaced them in the West. For the basic economic unit in modern China is the self-supporting commune, encouraging the dispersal of industrial effort; while her gigantic system of inland waterways, developed over the centuries (the Peking-Hangchow canal, linking two cities as far apart as London and Athens, was started in 1287), continues to provide cheap transport and, thanks to the major engineering developments of recent years, an important source of hydro-electric power.

Pandas made of strong cotton crochet by women in village commune workshops.

Right: Chinese children playing traditional instruments.

A prized jet aeroplane in a Peking street.

Chinese paper flowers—which used to bloom in London too: "In Leather Lane and Shepherd's Bush . . . men would each cry one particular line—it might be gay paper hats, or sunshades . . . Sometimes their trays would blossom with Chinese flowers, a miracle of ingenuity, which would change from a fan to a flower, and from a flower to three complex balls of folded paper, meanwhile shading from violet to blue, from orange to crimson in a carnival of colour enough to challenge any rainbow that ever spanned those dingy London roofs." (Lesley Gordon "A Peepshow into Paradise", 1953).

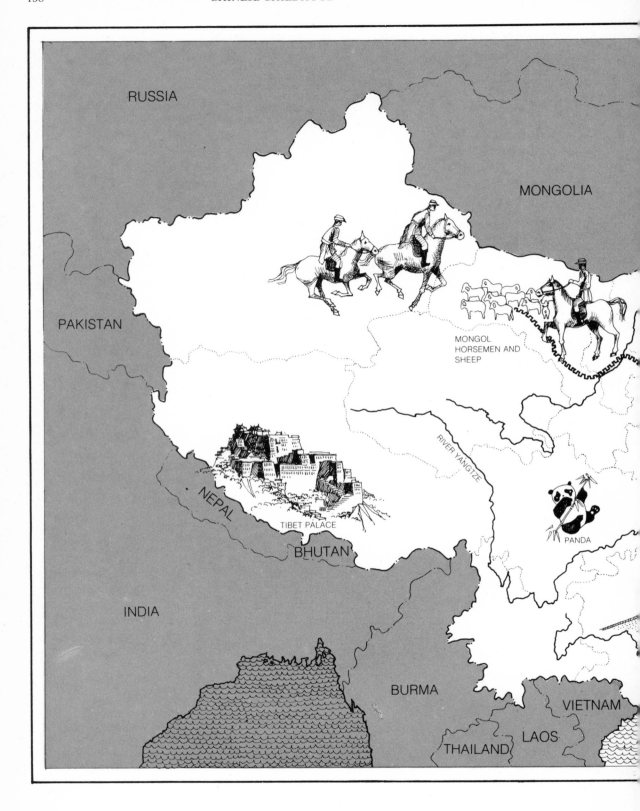

RUSSIA

MONGOLIA

PAKISTAN

MONGOL
HORSEMEN AND
SHEEP

RIVER YANGTZE

NEPAL

TIBET PALACE

BHUTAN

PANDA

INDIA

BURMA

VIETNAM

LAOS

THAILAND

*Map of China drawn by
Kwok Siu Wing.*

GREAT WALL

PEKING

PALACE

EKING MAN

SILKWORMS

KOREA

JAPAN

SHANGHAI

POTTERY

LDS AND BUFFALO

TAIWAN

CANTON

HONG KONG

N
NW NE
W E
SW SE
S

Stamp collecting, a favourit
hobby with Chinese children
recent issues of stamps
depicting toys and children
playing.

CHAPTER ELEVEN

CHINESE TRIFLES

*In which are examined the figurines
in the Peking market, yesterday and today,
and their derivation from funerary cult-objects.
And in which is told the story of Lou Pan the Master
Mason, and how he transformed the minions
of the Dragon King into the fantastic
roof decorations familiar today.*

In the autumn of 1936, before the Japanese invasion of China, Lady Dorothea Hosie was staying at an old-fashioned school for girls in Peking run by two rather fierce Chinese ladies. Occasionally they relaxed and took her shopping or to visit the Temple Fairs.

"My favourite pursuit," writes Lady Dorothea in her book 'The Pool of Ch'ien Lung', "was to loiter in the Eastern Peace Market, and choose from the stalls a selection of the myriad diminutive clay toys there displayed. One could acquire a whole wedding procession, marvellously fashioned; or a farmer with his hoe, perfectly proportioned; a priest reading his sutra; a musician in a long robe eternally blowing on his flute; a fisherman for ever dangling his optimist's rod; a boy happily kicking his shuttlecock with the flat of his heel. Or two old men with thin, silky white beards sitting cross-legged and earnest over their chess; a general, painted and beplumed, brandishing his sword; or the smiling god of old age holding his rosy pomegranate in one hand while he leans on his gnarled stick with the other. The whole of society packed with cotton wool and carried home in half-a-dozen match-boxes."

These tiny clay figurines are dressed in the regional costumes of some of the minority ethnic groups who live in China today and whose language and culture differs substantially from those of Peking.

Left: A cart made of pottery. Han Dynasty (206 BC — 220 AD). In the British Museum.
Below left: A model of a house made of pottery, Han Dynasty (206 — 220 AD). In the British Museum.
Below right: Tomb figure of dancer made of pottery, 6 Dynasties type (220 — 479 AD) but probably recent. In the British Museum.

Forty years on, past wars, social revolution and vast political upheavals the little clay market figures are still selling well. They decorate a new set of postage stamps issued in 1974 by the Post Office of the People's Republic of China; and throughout the world they grace the shelves of bookshops selling 'China Reconstructs' and 'The Thoughts of Chairman Mao'—just as in the past they cluttered up the glass-fronted curio cabinets of our great-grandmothers. Indeed one might argue that they have been a good selling line in China for the past three or four thousand years; for are not today's 'Chinese Trifles', or those little figurines, knick-knacks, tiny pagodas, rustic pavilions and glass menageries curiously akin to the statuettes, urns, bronze horses and chariots that the great princes and princesses of China had buried with them, once they gave up the more ancient, more barbaric and more wasteful practice of burying wives, slaves, concubines and other costly goods and chattels inside their massive tombs?

Village occupations: boxwood carvings made in a southern Chinese Christian mission 40 years ago. The boxwood tree is admirable for carving, but rarely grows more than a few inches in diameter. In the province of Kiangsu and Fukien, this wood is used traditionally to make small carvings of everyday objects.

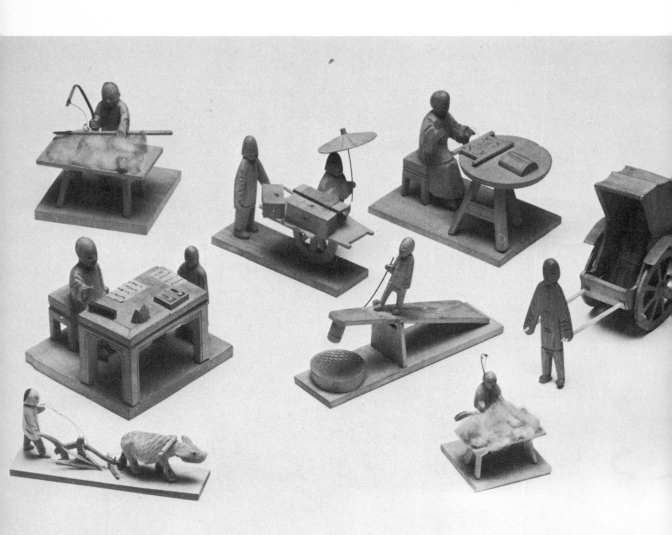

*Left: Bronze ritual vessel
"yu", Chou Dynasty
11 — 10th century BC.*

*Below: Bronze toy teaset
bought in Shanghai, 1920.*

Lou Pan, the Master Carpenter

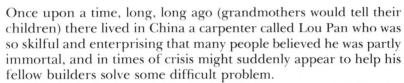

A green glazed pottery watch tower, 33 inches high, made in China two thousand years ago. In the British Museum.

Once upon a time, long, long ago (grandmothers would tell their children) there lived in China a carpenter called Lou Pan who was so skilful and enterprising that many people believed he was partly immortal, and in times of crisis might suddenly appear to help his fellow builders solve some difficult problem.

Now when the Emperor was re-building the palace at Peking he commanded (so they say) that towers should be built at every corner, each tower having three tiers of elaborate roofs.

"How can we build square towers each with three separate roofs?" lamented the builders. Day in and day out they discussed the problem, but could find no solution.

The most worried of all was Wu, their chief, as he was directly responsible to the Emperor. Weary and depressed, he made his way home oblivious of all the noise and gaiety of the market place; yet as he neared his house he became aware of a stall he had never seen before set up a few yards from his door. An old man was selling singing birds and cages: he stepped out in front of Wu and begged him most insistently to stop and buy one of his pretty cages.

Wu brushed him aside rather crossly; but just as he was about to enter his house, he ran back and hurriedly bought the beautiful cage the man was holding out to him. He had suddenly realised it was a square cage of wickerwork with three layers of roofs, making 36 elegant ridges . . . The birdman and his stall were never seen again.

Yet there were times, so the stories go, when Lou Pan himself, when he was alive, had to call for outside help. It happened to him one day when he wished to build himself a new house, and could not think what to do.

"The Dragon King has just built himself a superb new palace," said one of Lou Pan's apprentices. "Perhaps if you had a look at it it might give you a few ideas."

"Perhaps," said Lou Pan, and off he went to see the Dragon King —and managed to talk him into lending him the beautiful new palace for three whole days. It was indeed a splendid building: bright, golden rooms with elegant red pillars supporting roofs of sea-green tiles which glistened and shone like the iridescent waves of the sea.

Quickly Lou Pan and his apprentices dismantled the elegant palace and took it to his domain; and there, for three days and three nights, they laboured to erect it again. They had just put the last tile in place when far away a rushing, roaring sound was heard in the night sky.

"Quick, quick," shouted Lou Pan, "fetch strong ropes and peg the building down at all four corners!" while he himself climbed up and fixed four bells under the eaves.

There was a rush like a hurricane; and all the young dragons, lobsters, fishes and shrimps sent by the king to carry his palace home started to push and pull with all their strength. But though they heaved and tugged till cock-crow they could not move it an inch, so securely had Lou Pan anchored it down; and as dawn broke all the dragons, lobsters, fishes and shrimps turned to stone. And there they remained.

They looked so fine, straining away on the roof-tops and gables, that Lou Pan's disciples and descendants have continued to this day to ornament their houses in just that way.

A recent photograph taken in Taiwan of Chinese glazed roof tiles.

Dolls in China

The absence until quite recent times of little girls' playthings such as dolls, dolls' houses, cradles and miniature furniture has been commented on by several historians of Chinese social customs—notably by G. Schlegel in a thesis on Chinese toys and pastimes presented to the University of Jena in 1869. Schlegel, who had been a Chinese interpreter in the service of the Dutch government in Batavia, states that:

"In the Chinese and Korean languages the word 'doll' comes from the same root as the words for 'idol' and 'fetish'. Little girls in China never play with dolls, which are regarded as having magical power."

It is not our purpose here to delve into the realms of magic images, votive figures, talismans, fetishes, idols, amulets, ancestor-worship, grave furniture, and funeral sacrifices. These matters have been fully examined by Max von Boehn in his book 'Dolls and Puppets', first published in 1920. It is interesting to note, however, Schlegel's finding that in Japan too dolls as playthings were unknown before the arrival of the Dutch. Until then they had been used as talismans against illness and, as in China, as ritual objects to be held during confinement, or placed as a temple offering when one hoped for the birth of a child.

Little figures in a miniature Chinese garden. In "Six Chapters of a Floating Life" the writer Chen Fou, who was born in 1763, gives a charming account of how he and his wife made a pretty little garden on a plate, left it out on the window sill overnight and how two fighting cats fell and broke it. His advice on growing miniature plants, arranging flowers and landscaping a tiny backyard are as relevant today as they were 200 years ago.

Stand up Little Priest, and the germ of a Million Rouble Industry.

These little dolls have a weight in the base; however hard they are pushed over, they roll back to an upright position. This type of doll is also made in large quantities in Japan, where it is called a 'Daruma'. It is said to represent a Buddhist monk who sat absorbed in his Zen meditations for so long that his limbs withered away. Children sometimes draw him with only one eye; make a wish; and if the wish comes true, paint in the other eye.

Mrs. Poynter, who lived in Shanghai until she was married, remembers that when she was a little girl she and her sisters used to play with some rather flattened, egg-shaped little bodies in lacquer-ware, which opened up, revealing a whole series of bodies fitting one inside the other, until the last tiny one opened and there was a minute glass bead. "We thought they were Russian," said Mrs. Poynter, "as they came from Harbin."

Could these be the same little toys mentioned by Manfred Bachmann and Claus Hausmann in 'Dolls the World Over', when they are speaking of the million-rouble Soviet industry of wooden 'matreshka' nesting dolls?

"This special type of doll," they say, "came to Russia from the Far East at the turn of the century, when Moscow enthusiasts of folk art had a model made by the master turner W. Svyosdochkin from sketches made by the painter S. Malyutin. Their production was taken up in a centre of toy-making close to the monastery of Troize-Sergiyevsky, now the town of Sagorsk, near Moscow. Early in the 19th century there were sets of dolls in China, thinly turned and grotesquely lacquered: the innermost kernel of these was a tiny bud or a bird's egg, according to the flower- or bird-myths of that region."

Chinese Animals and the Cycle of Years

Chinese foxes, like foxes the world over, are sly and cunning. They are also fond of a drop of wine, and are often to be found lurking in the bushes near inns and taverns. Chinese vixens, as many folk tales recount, enjoy disguising themselves as bewitching young ladies, beguiling solitary travellers returning home in the midnight hours.

Chinese hares and rabbits are protected by a distinguished relative who lives up in the moon. Tortoises, because of their long lives, are reputed to be very wise and able to foresee the future: with the dragon, the phoenix and the unicorn they helped the Creator to transform primaeval chaos into sky and earth.

Until quite recently country people divided days and nights into twelve two-hour periods each bearing the name of an animal. The secret midnight hours of 11pm to 1am are the Hours of the Rat. The time of the ox is 1am to 3am, a time of rest, of gentle kindness

Claymen with feet of lead and papier maché lion who won't lie down.

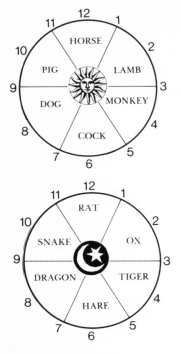

The animal cycle of the day and the years.

and sweetness for all dumb, patient, hard-working toilers in the fields. The early dawn, from 3 to 5 o'clock, sees the tiger, the king of the beasts, rising up fiercely to renew his strength, to attack and devour all demons and evil things. At 5, the crafty and wise old hare comes down from the moon and presides over the morning hours until at 7 o'clock the Dragon, lord and monarch of all living things, begins his reign. This lasts until at 9 his lowly relation, the snake, takes over, crawling through the next stretch—hiding in the grass, plotting nasty tricks, and on occasion turning himself and his friends into apparently saintly little housewives. Between 11 and 1 o'clock, out in the midday sun the horse, brave and patient, exhausts his great strength. The last five periods of the day are devoted to the lamb, the monkey, the cock, the dog and the pig.

As in Europe, Chinese dogs are brave, loyal and faithful; while sheep, docile and meek, go quietly to their doom. Chinese children were constantly reminded that dutiful sons and daughters should kneel like little lambs before their respected parents.

The cock, who dominates the late afternoon from 5 to 7pm, is admired for his manly, military virtues. He fights resolutely facing the enemy, claws sharp, comb and tail erect; he shares his food generously with his companions; and with unfailing regularity he announces the arrival of new dawns, new hopes, new aspirations. He is the symbol of many New Year messages and greetings.

The hours of the pig, from 9 to 11 in the evening, are hours of greed, of money, of lust, and of all that is base in human nature; while the best-loved of all Chinese animals, the monkey, disports himself in the heyday of the afternoon—mischievously flitting between heaven and earth, turning everything topsy-turvy, untamed, unbound, symbol of man's free, creative intelligence.

This Chinese pattern of the hours is repeated in the twelve-year cycle of the old Chinese calendar. Boys playing leap-frog chanted a Chinese tongue-twister going something like this: "One for the Rat, Two for the Ox, Three for the Tiger, Four for the Hare . . . . . . " Anyone making a mistake became the "frog".

The recurring cycle of twelve years explains why Chinese babies are considered to be one year old as soon as they are born. Ages are reckoned by the annual animal signs: thus, anyone born, for example, between the first and the last days of the Year of the Dragon becomes two years old immediately the Year of the Snake, which follows it, begins.

CHAPTER TWELVE

OMBRES CHINOISES

*Of Chinoiserie abroad: Of the
Chinese shadow-theatre and its adoption
in Paris; of the world-wide reverberations of the
Siege of Peking; of Chinese dolls in California,
the Willow Pattern Plate in England,
Pandas in the London Zoo, and
the long reign of Prince Aladdin.*

Above: "Le Boxer Vaincu" and "La Guerre en Chine"—two "gentils jeux de société," as the publisher calls them, in which the players draw lots to determine which army of occupation—German, British, Russian, American or Japanese—each shall represent.

In the middle of the 18th century it became fashionable in Europe to have the outline of one's face or figure cut out of black paper and mounted on a pale background. These silhouette pictures became so popular that an enterprising Italian showman called Chiarini contrived to put together an entertainment of moving shadows with which he toured the capitals of Europe. He was no doubt inspired by what he had seen, or heard, of Chinese shadow puppets, for he called his performance 'Ombres Chinoises'.

These shadow plays caught the imagination of many talented Europeans. In 1781 Goethe had a shadow theatre built for himself; while a Berlin theatre established a complete repertoire of romantic shadow dramas.

In Paris, from 1881 onwards, the café 'Le Chat Noir' became a meeting place for writers and artists who amused themselves watching the magical effects produced by Henri Rivière's skilful use of lights, colour transparencies and poetical shadow figures. And soon after, Parisian toyshops were offering for sale all kinds of 'Théâtres d'Ombres' featuring vaguely oriental figures, or cut-out books such as 'La Prise de Pékin'.

La Prise de Pékin

This publication by Hachette, with music by Gaston Meynard, illustrations by R. de la Nezière and text by J. Jacquin, gives instructions on how to set up and perform the play. The play itself tells the quite improbable story of how two French soldiers get mixed up with a circus run by a stage comic Italian, a French-speaking Chinese Lord High Executioner and his pretty daughter Iris Blossom. It ends with the triumphal entry of the French army into Peking and the French hero of this patriotic fantasy taking Iris back to Paris with him.

The historical reality on which these events were based was very much grimmer. Exasperated by the follies of the Manchu reaction-

Below: Funeral Procession. This represents the funeral procession of the last Manchu Emperor Kuang Hsu who died in 1908. In 1898 he had prepared a number of far reaching reforms, but was prevented from carrying them out by the Dowager Empress Tz'u-Hsi. From then on Kuang Hsu was no more than a puppet emperor. The procession was made in 1909, by the firm of G.B.G.Gerbeau in Paris, who specialised in lead toys.

aries and by the greed of foreign powers (including France and England) who had obtained land and trade concessions in China, many patriotic Chinese formed secret societies whose aim was to reform the Chinese government and get rid of the foreigners.

In 1900 the secret society of the Boxers surrounded the Legation Quarter of Peking, where all foreign residents lived, and kept up the siege for 50 days. The barricades were not lifted till an Expeditionary Force consisting of soldiers from seven Western powers entered Peking and occupied the Imperial Palace. The Chinese were forced to pay a large indemnity and to agree to foreign powers being allowed to build railways and run the ports, the mines and many other lucrative enterprises.

In Europe these events unleashed a new wave of interest in chinoiseries and exotic oriental objects. Smart Parisian ladies stuck chrysanthemums into pots and fans on to screens, read novels by Pierre Loti and bought their children Chinese-style shadow puppets to play with and Chinese paper pagodas and pavilions to cut out and build, such as those published by Pellerin at Epinal.

Chinese fortified gateway, made in England.

Two-faced Mandarins: turn the book upside down to see his other face. Paris, early 20th century.

Meanwhile in Germany an old-established family of pewter and tinsmiths, Babette Schweizer of Diessen near Munich, were bringing their famous tin soldiers up to date by making moulds of German soldiers and Boxer revolutionaries slaughtering each other.

Oriental Babies

In the first decade of this century a new type of doll began to appear on the display shelves of toyshops. Side by side with beautifully dressed, ideally pretty little girl dolls there were now offered for sale New Born Babes, realistically modelled from life, little Red Indian Squaws, Oriental and Black Babies.

These dolls, neatly dressed in fringed deerskin, exotic kimonos, or plantation cottons, were not 'tourist souvenirs' as we know them, but the current products of most European manufacturers adapted to meet the growing demand for 'character dolls'. Brown and yellow pigments were added; the line of the eyebrows altered; the style of hair changed—yet basically these dolls remained akin to all the others produced in the factory, whether they were made by Bru, Jumeau, Steiner, Kestner, Armand Marseille or anyone else.

These 'oriental babies' which have survived the past 50 years have nearly always had the brocaded jacket or kimono removed, and been re-dressed in long, lace-trimmed, embroidered baby-clothes. The dolls representing little girls, however, often wear long-sleeved kimono-type garments, suggesting a possible inspiration from 'Madame Butterfly'.

An "oriental" baby doll. Designed by Julio Kilenyi, for the American firm of Louis Amberg, and made in Germany in 1910. Has a china head and composition body.

Mrs. Coleman, in her authoritative 'Encyclopaedia of Dolls', lists some European dolls made in 1897 which had bisque heads and wooden bodies, and were dressed in clothes of Chinese style. They cost, wholesale, 8 dollars per dozen for the 10 inch size and 17 dollars for the 12 inch.

By 1909 a new breed of doll had appeared, with soft bodies stuffed with cork and supposedly unbreakable heads made out of a mixture of glue, chemicals and wood or paper pulp. "Can't Break 'em" they were called by one giant American importing firm, Horseman & Co.

The moulding process—more flexible and cheaper than what was involved in producing bisque and china heads—turned doll-making into a mass-production industry, constantly on the look-out for titillating 'novelties', for crazes to promote and advertising campaigns to latch on to.

China was quaint, so China duly got the treatment. Between 1911 and 1917 Horseman & Co. commissioned Helen Trowbridge to design a whole series of dolls for them: she responded with 'Peterkin', 'Pippin', 'Rosebud' and many others including (it was one of the first) 'Chinkee', based on one of her own paintings: a cute little Chinese baby with pink and green satin jacket, black trousers and slippers. In 1915 followed the 'Canton Kids', modelled on two children from San Francisco's Chinatown.

There are other dolls of the same period which, accidentally as it were, have a slight air of the orient about them. When, during the 1914-18 War, American firms were unable to get dolls from Germany, they set about having them made in Japan. The Japanese craftsmen employed to make the moulds copied every detail of the models before them—even such details as 'Made in Germany'; yet their earlier products had a slight, but unmistakable Japanese aura. However the big American-Japanese firms like Morimura soon rectified this, and ended up by making Japan for a time the largest exporter of dolls in the world.

Figure from a French board-game. Paris, early 20th century.

The Willow Pattern Plate

If any oriental baby doll wanted to sit down to a quiet cup of tea, what could be more suitable than a tea-set decorated with the pretty willow pattern?

This is the story of the little Chinese figures who are running over the bridge. The first one is a beautiful young girl, Koing-Se. She is followed by her lover, Chang. They are running away from the rich old mandarin, her father, who lives in the ornate pagoda next to the willow tree. On the other side of the bridge is the poor home of a gardener where the lovers find a temporary refuge. They manage by skill and daring to escape by boat and sail away to the Yangtse-Kiang River, where they settle on the little island at the top of the picture. But the nasty old father and the rich Duke who wants to marry his pretty daughter discover their retreat.

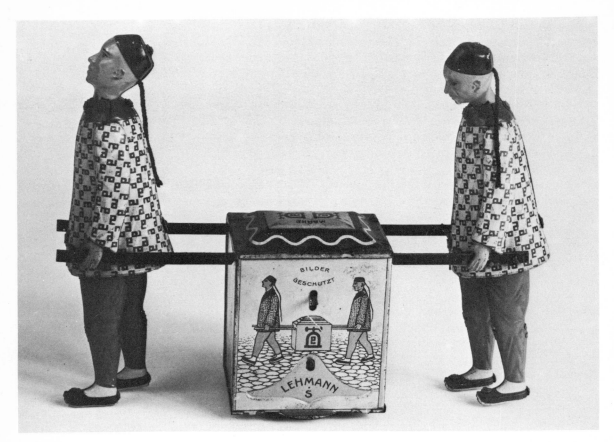

Clockwork toy, made by the German firm Lehmann.

Chang is brutally murdered and Koing-Se in despair rushes into the house, which she sets on fire, and perishes in the flames. The lovers are transformed into the two doves flying in the sky— symbols of love and constancy.

The willow pattern originated at the Caughley porcelain factory in Shropshire, in about 1780. It is an English adaptation of the kind of river scene depicted on porcelain made in China for export.

The custom of tea drinking came to Europe from China in the 17th century. The Chinese had for many centuries been drinking an infusion of the green leaves of the tea bush as a kind of medicine which they hoped would help prolong life.

Pandas for Britain from China with Love

So ran the newspaper headlines in the summer of 1974 when Mr. Edward Heath arrived back from a visit to China with the news that two giant pandas, Ching-Ching ('crystal bright') and Chia-Chia ('most excellent and very best') were coming to England as a gift of the Chinese people.

Pandas are one of the world's rarest animals: they live quiet, solitary lives in the misty bamboo groves of Swechwan's remote and inaccessible mountains. Until 1938 very few people in England had ever heard of a panda, and in China itself it was a mysterious animal that had only been seen by one or two intrepid hunters. For thousands of years Chinese artists had used the elegant patterns of bamboo leaves as a recurrent theme, yet no picture of a panda had been made until quite recent times.

In 1938 three pandas which had been captured by an Englishman, Lloyd Tangier Smith, arrived in London. Only the baby, Ming, survived captivity, and she soon became as popular as any film star. She did not sleep at the zoo, but arrived each day by car, sitting in front with the driver and waving her paw to the crowds. And soon the toyshops of England were full of little stuffed, furry pandas.

When war came it became difficult to feed Ming, so a public appeal by radio was made on her behalf. As a result, ample supplies were found in Cornwall; and these were also used to feed her successor at the zoo, the mischievous Chi-Chi, who was dearly loved by all until she died in 1972. Indeed her only fault was to ignore the attentions of An-An, who was brought from Russia at great expense to keep her company.

For the last 15 years the Polkerris Boy Scout Troop have made it their business to keep the London pandas well supplied with Cornish bamboo.

"Hovis" a well loved panda, now 18 years old.

Prince Aladdin: an old Chinese acquaintance?

Our grandchildren have invited us to the play. The rather battered toy theatre which has already served three generations of children has been re-furbished; and we are to see (so says the programme note) the 'Grand Romantic Spectacle of Aladdin' as first performed at the Theatre Royal, Covent Garden in 1826.

"Scene 1: A Street in China." The miniature footlights glow in the dark, the cardboard curtain rises jerkily to the strains of 'In a Persian Market', and against a brilliant backcloth of minarets and arched Turkish gateways stands the wicked magician Abanazar crying "New Lamps for Old!" Mustapha the widow scolds her idle son and the six-year-old voice replies firmly: "Don't worry mother. I'll bring you a feast—and then . . . . . . and then I'm going to marry the Emperor's daughter."

Abanazar . . . . Mustapha . . . . Kazim Azac . . . . These are not Chinese names; yet whether Aladdin and the Wonderful Lamp is performed on a cardboard stage or at the local repertory theatre there is always a 'Chinese' element which clings to it—more robust and funnier than the traditional European 18th century 'chinoiserie'.

This theatrical tradition is echoed in the story-books. There is the same strange mixture of Sultans, Grand Viziers and Emperors; at one moment the wicked African magician leaves Persia for good; at another we are with Aladdin in China, peeping at the

"Peepshow, a Street in China", cut-out published in 1909 by the Church of England Zenana Missionary Society.
In a booklet which accompanied the cardboard sheets, Blanche Cooper gave informative details of the shops, opium dens and characters in the model. She suggested that viewers should be charged a penny a peep, to collect funds for the missionary work among the poor heathen Chinese.

beautiful princess on her way to the Public Baths—and this without any of the genie's magical tricks. To elucidate it all, shall we be obliged to ferret out a copy of 'Les Mille et Une Nuits', as published by the French ambassador at Constantinople, M. Antoine Galland, in Paris in 1704; or one of the early chapbooks containing an English translation of this immensely popular collection of stories? Or consult, in the British Library, all eleven volumes of Richard Burton's translation from the Arabic, which includes all the verses and "bits only suitable for Arabs and old gentlemen," as Andrew Lang says in the preface to his own familiar version of the 'Arabian Nights'? As we reflect on the origins and identity of our childhood acquaintance Prince Aladdin, through whom many young children have acquired their first vague awareness of the existence of a place called 'China', the words "Tahi Tongluck, Emperor of Tartary" on the toy theatre programme catch our eye. They bring back long forgotten echoes of school lessons, jigsaw odds and ends of information and knowledge . . . . Of course there was a time, to which we can give precise historical dates, when an idle young boy in Baghdad could dream of finding fame and fortune in far-off China, and with resolution could set about doing just that. Did not the great Mongol conqueror Genghis Khan himself marry a Chinese princess? Did not the vast empire he handed on stretch, soon after his death, from Peking to Budapest? Had not Mongol armies occupied Poland and Russia, and only been stopped on their way to the River Jordan by the fierce defence of the Egyptian Mamelukes at the siege of Aleppo? His grandson Kubla Khan had become Emperor of all China and founder of the Yuan Dynasty; another grandson ruled Persia; other descendants, Turkestan and Russia.

During all this time there was interchange of skills, commerce, ideas. The Chinese taught the Mongols engineering; how to use smoke screens, gunpowder and siege engines in war; and in peace to wear silk and live in civilised ease. China learned from Persia and the Middle East how to make knotted carpets, and the blue cobalt which they afterwards used for the famous blue and white porcelain made in the province of Kiang-si. From the Mongol invaders she acquired fine horses, skill in archery, the game of polo; and with them she built the stable economy which made possible such vast engineering works as the Grand Canal between the Yellow River and the Yangtse-Kiang. Cargo ships bound for Java, Ceylon and India filled the great Chinese ports; while innumerable caravans set out on the overland routes which linked China with the West.

Miss Vincent as Prince Aladdin: a theatrical portrait published by J. Fairburn, Jan 1837.

Below: Toy Theatre characters from a sheet published in 1831 by C. Hodgson.

Kalim Azack   Zuma   Aladdin entombed in the Cave   Kayarack

Amron   Combat Kalim Azack & Kayarack   Abanazare 2nd Dress

Published Dec.r 12th 1831 by C.Hodgson 10 Cloth Fair London

Envoi - The Scroll - Again

Heaven wants children throughout the world to grow up like the ideal
    boys on the scroll: they are not mortal, but symbols of children fed
on the milk of heaven. Like the dragon, the phoenix, the tortoise, the
    Ch'i-Lin, they are visible symbols of spiritual truths.
If we study the lotus and gather the cinnamon flowers of knowledge,
    peace will reign in the world. Therefore boys should learn good
manners, music and poetry as well as chess, archery and horsemanship;
    so that when they grow up they will be fit in mind and body and
excel in intellectual and in practical fields.

         Lin Shang-chen of the Ming.

One of the five poems and commentaries by five different
scholars written at the end of the scroll of 'A Hundred Sons'.

校圖于群衆遞見犀兒
戲坐以異亍立行裸袒及
別妣鱗 介羽炱中紛
牝孃眞僞州木刿荇
芳拳緣浮呈致凡有
不悟情授皆兲藝兂
兩恋訊書不失青靈老
林子友祿題

A Further Scholarly Comment

The opening chapter of the *"Men of the Marshes"*, a 14th century epic tale of Chinese outlaws and Robin Hoods, recounts how a quick-witted, unscrupulous fellow gets on in the world and finally lands the job of War Minister, by means of his remarkable skill at kicking a football.

Chia Pao-yu, the hero of the great 18th century novel of manners *"Dream of a Red Chamber"*, spends a lot of time in the company of his pretty cousins — playing Go, solving metal puzzles, making up riddles and word-games, collecting and arranging flowers, painting, writing poetry, singing songs and playing his Chinese guitar.

There are many other references to toys, games and pastimes in Chinese literature. Yu-ying Brown of the Department of Oriental Antiquities of the British Library has made out, from her wide reading of Chinese books, this short list of some of the earliest written records of Chinese toys and childhood pastimes:

CHAPTER I

Acrobat (Fan chin-to)
Date:
First recorded in *Chan-kuo ts'e*, the history of the Warring States period (480 — 221 BC). But actual Acrobatics as we know it was not established till 5th — 6th century AD.
Source:
Huang Hua-chieh's *Chung-kuo min-chien pai-hsi*. Popular games and entertainments in Chinese history. (Taipei, 1967).

Judo (Ch'uan-fa)
Date:
10th century.
Source:
Wu-tai shih, the history of the Five dynasties.

Wrestling (Hsiang-p'u)
Date:
3rd century BC.
Source:
Ssu-Ma Ch'ien's *Shih-chi*, the history of pre-Han China.

CHAPTER II

Fire-crackers (Pao-chu)
Date:
Han dynasty.

Fireworks (Yen-huo)
Date:
7th century AD.
Source:
Wang Chi's *Shih-wu yuan-hui*, the origin of things and matters, Chapter 37. (1797).

CHAPTER IV

Diabolo (K'ung-chung)
Date:
17th century.
Source:
Ti-ching ching-wu-lueh, description of Peking and its environs, published in 1635.

Football (Ts'u-chu)
Date:
The Warring States period (480 — 221 BC)
Source:
Han-shu i-wen-chi, bibliography of early Han works, compiled by Pan Ku (d. 92 AD). In this bibliography, *Ts'u-chu ching*, the way of football, is listed.

Kite-flying (Fang chih-yuan)
Date:
2nd century BC.
Source:
Chung-kuo min-chien pai-hsi, op. cit., pp.153 — 163

Skipping (T'iao sheng)
Date:
6th century.
Source:
Tsung Lin's *Ching ch'u sui-shih-chi*, a calendar of popular customs throughout the year.
Remarks:
Established as a children's game since the 7th century.

Shuttlecocks (Chien-tzu)
Date:
19th century. The Empress Dowager Tz'ui Hsi (1835 — 1909) caused her courtiers to play the game.
Source:
Nagao Tatsuzo's *Shina minzoku-shi*, manners and customs of the Chinese. (Tokyo, 1940 — 42) Vol. 2, p.707.

Stilts (Kao-chiao)
Date:
3 — 4th century BC.
Source:
Lieh-Tzu, a Taoist philisophical work attributed to Lieh-Tzu (c. 4th century BC).
Remarks:
This game became popular during the Sung dynasty; and it has been played mainly in North China as a New Year pastime.

Tops (T'o-lei)
Date:
17th century
Source:
The name T'o-lei first appeared in Liu T'ung and Yu I-cheng's *Ti-ching ching-wu-lueh*. op.cit.

Whistles (Hsiao-tzu)
Date:
17th century. Recorded by Wang Shih-chen (1634 — 1711), in his *Chu-i lu*, anecdotes relating to the early Ch'ing period.
Source:
Tun-ch'ung's *Yen-ching sui-shih-chi*, annual customs and festivals in Peking, published in 1900. This book has been translated into English by Derk Bodde. (Hong Kong University Press, 1965, second edition).

Windmills (Feng ch'e)
Date:
17th century.
Source:
Ti-ching ching-wu-lueh, op.cit.

CHAPTER V

Chess (Hsiang-ch'i, i.e. "elephant checkers")
Date:
10 — 11th century.
Source:
T'ai-p'ing yu-lan, a Sung encyclopaedia.

Go (Wei-ch'i, i.e. "surrounding checkers")
Date:
7th century AD. (Some said it was invented by Emperor Jao (c. 2356 BC) for his son).
Source:
T'ai-p'ing yu-lan, op.cit.

Puzzles (Mi-yu)
Date:
3rd century AD.
Source:
Liu Hsieh's *Wen-hsin tiao-lung*, critic on literature.

Sheng-kuan t'u (the game of promotion)
Description:
This is played on a board or plan representing an official career from the lowest to the highest grade, according to the imperial examination system. It is a kind of Snakes and Ladders, played with four dice; the object of each player being to secure promotion over the others.
Date:
7th century AD.
Source:
Shina minzoku-shi, op.cit.

CHAPTER VI

Hobby-horse (Chu-ma)
Date and source:
First recorded in *Hou-Han shu*, the chronicle of the Later Han dynasty (25 — 220 AD). See the section on the biography of T'ao Chi'en, who was seen playing the toy at the age of fourteen. He later became a very famous general.

CHINA		REST OF THE WORLD
	巨猿人	

1,000,000 B.C. — GIANT APE — 巨猿人 — AUSTRALOPITHECUS / MAN LIVED IN AFRICA / ICE AGE IN EUROPE

900,000 B.C.

800,000 B.C.

700,000 B.C.

600,000 B.C. — SKULL OF LANTIEN MAN (FOUND 1964) MADE SIMPLE TOOLS, COOKED FOOD — 藍田人

500,000 B.C. — PEKING MAN — 北京人

400,000 B.C.

300,000 B.C.

200,000 B.C. — EARLY NEANDERTHAL MAN IN EUROPE

100,000 B.C. — UPPER CAVE MEN

50,000 B.C. — 穴居人 — CRO MAGNON IN FRANCE

20,000 B.C. — LASCAUX CAVE PAINTING

CHINA | REST OF THE WORLD

	CHINA		REST OF THE WORLD
10,000 B.C.			ADAM AND EVE
9,000 B.C.			
8,000 B.C.	BOWS AND ARROWS POTTERY VESSELS FOR COOKING FARMING	弓 箭 農	STONE AGE
7,000 B.C.			THE FLOOD
6,000 B.C.			
5,000 B.C.	POTTERY PITCHER FOR WATER	陶 盆 水 罐 灌 溉 文 字	UR
4,000 B.C.	LEGENDARY EMPEROR TAMED YELLOW RIVER STARTED IRRIGATION INVENTED WRITING		EGYPT — FIRST DYNASTY
3,000 B.C.	SILK WEAVING TIMBER HOUSES BOATS	蠶 桑 舟 居	PYRAMIDS
2,000 B.C.	LACQUER INVENTED BRONZE CASTING FIRST CHINESE BOOK	銅 器 漆 器 孔 子 長 城 造 紙	STONEHENGE KNOSSOS MYCENAE TROJAN WAR
		商 SHANG	
1,000 B.C.	FOOTBALL, KITES ABACUS, WHEELBARROW CONFUCIUS, MECH. TOYS IRON USED CHOPSTICKS GREAT WALL BUILT DRAGON BOAT FESTIVAL	周 CHOU	PHOENICIAN ALPHABET 1st. OLYMPIAD MARATHON ALEXANDER CLEOPATRA JULIUS CAESAR MURDERED HANNIBAL CROSSES ALPS
0		漢 HAN	JESUS CHRIST
200 A.D.	PAPER INVENTED MAGIC SQUARE		ST. PAUL NERO
500 A.D.	TOPS		CONSTANTINE ALARIC SACKS ROME

	CHINA				EUROPE
	EVENTS	TOY OR GAME		DYNASTY	
500 A.D	FIRST CAST IRON BRIDGE		鑄鐵橋	唐 TANG	ST. AUGUSTINE
600					
700		CHESS WEI CHI	象棋圍棋、煙花、柔道、		ARABS INVADE SPAIN, FRANCE MAHOMET
800	PRINTING INVENTED	FIREWORKS			CHARLEMAGNE ALFRED
900	MOVABLE TYPE GUNPOWDER	SNAKES & LADDERS JUDO	印染術、火藥、活版		
1,000				宋 SUNG	BATTLE OF HASTINGS ROLAND & OLIVER DOMESDAY
1,100		CARDS	紙牌、		MURDER OF BECKET ST. LOUIS FIRST CRUSADE
1,200	GENGHIZ KHAN MARCO POLO IN CHINA		成吉斯汗、通商申畫百科全書、	元 MONGOL EMPIRE	MAGNA CARTA DANTE & BEATRICE SPAGHETTI
1,300	ARAB & JEWISH MERCHANTS TRADE WITH CHINA	CANNON PUZZLES WITH RINGS		明 MING	BLACK DEATH
1,400	GREAT ENCYCLOPEDIA CHANG HO'S VOYAGES	TEMPLE OF HEAVEN FOLDING FAN		摺扇 風車 葡紙、	AGINCOURT JOAN OF ARC GUTENBERG TURKS CAPTURE CONSTANTINOPLE CHRISTOPHER COLUMBUS
1,500		DIABOLO WINDMILLS SHUTTLECOCKS			HENRY VIII CESARE BORGIA ELIZABETH I SHAKESPEARE
1,600	JESUITS IN CHINA ORANGES & PAGODA PAPERS TO EUROPE	PAPER CUTS	基督教傳入、	靖 MANCHU	SAVANA ROLA GUY FAWKES PUNCH & JUDY RICHELIEU GREAT FIRE OF LONDON LOUIS XIV
1,700	RHUBARB		鴉片戰爭、民國		POCOHONTAS FRENCH REVOLUTION MONTGOLFIER
1,800	FIRST OPIUM WAR TAI PING REBELLION	MAH-JONG	麻雀牌		NAPOLEON
1,900	BOXERS END OF MANCHU DYNASTY LONG MARCH CULTURE REVOLUTION			SUN YAT SEN PEOPLE'S REPUBLIC	

A HUNDRED BOOKS

Autobiographies

A Chinese Childhood.
Chiang Yee
Methuen & Co., London, 1946
Chinese Children at Play.
Yui Shu-Fang
Metheun & Co., London, 1936
The Crippled Tree/Birdless
Summer/A Mortal Flower. A trilogy.
Han Suyin
Granada Publishing Ltd., London,
1968
Le Palanquin des Larmes.
Chow Ching Lie
Editions Robert Laffont, Paris, 1975

Chinese Literature in Translation

Anthology of Chinese Literature.
Cyril Birch (ed.)
Penguin Books Ltd., London, 1975
170 Chinese Poems.
Arthur Waley (trans.)
Constable & Co., London, 1939
Eighteen Songs of a Nomad Flute.
The Story of Lady Wen-Chi.
Robert A. Role & Wen Fong
Metropolitan Museum of Art, New
York, 1974
Family.
Pa Chin
Doubleday & Co., New York, 1972
Monkey.
Wu Ch'eng-en (tr. A. Waley)
Penguin Books Ltd., London, 1961
The Perfect Lady by Mistake, and
other stories.
Feng Menglong (tr. William Dolby)
Elek Books Ltd., London, 1976
Recits d'une Vie Fugitive.
Jacques Reclus (trans.)
Gallimard, Paris, 1967
The Romance of the Western
Chamber.
T. C. Lai & Ed Gamarekian (trans.)
Heinemann Educational Books (Asia)
Ltd., Hong Kong, 1973
The Story of the Stone. vol. 1 The
Golden Days.
Cao Xueqin (trans. David Hawkes)
Penguin Books Ltd., London, 1973
Dream of the Red Chamber.
Chi-Chen Wang (trans.)
Vision Press Ltd., 1959
The Scholars.
Wu Ching-Tzu
Foreign Languages Press, Peking,
1973

Six Yuan Plays.
Liu Jung-en (trans.)
Penguin Books Ltd., London, 1972
Selected Stories of Lu Hsun
Yang Hsien-yi & Gladys Young (trans.)
Foreign Languages Press, Peking,
1960
Ten More Poems of Mao Tse-Tung.
Eastern Horizon Press, Hong Kong,
1967
Water Margin
Shih Nai-An (trans. J. H. Jackson)
Commercial Press Ltd., Hong Kong,
1963

The Siege of Peking

La Défense de la Legation de France
a Pekin.
Eugene Darcy
August Challamel, Paris, 1901
Les Derniers Jours de Pekin.
Pierre Loti
Calman-Levy, Paris, 1925
L'Enseigne de Vaisseau Paul Henry.
Rene Bazin
Tours, 1905
The Siege at Peking.
Peter Fleming
Rupert Hart-Davis, London, 1959
With the Allies to Peking.
G. A. Henty
Blackie & Son Ltd., London, 1903

Archaeology

Early Chinese Antiquities.
William Watson
Trustees of the British Museum,
London, 1950
The Genius of China.
William Watson
Times Newspapers Ltd., London,
1973
New Archaeological Finds in China.
Foreign Languages Press
Foreign Languages Press, Peking,
1974
Princes of Jade.
Edmond Capon & William Macquitty
Sphere Books, London, 1973

Science and Technology

China at Work.
Rudolf P. Hommel
M. I. T. Press, Cambs. Mass., 1969
La Conquete de l'Air.
A. van Hoorebeeck
Marabout Université, Verviers,
Belgium, 1967

Chinese Kites — How to make and fly
them.
David F. Jue
Charles E. Tuttle Co. Inc., Rutland
Vermont & Tokyo Japan, 1971
Kites.
Clive Bell
Faber & Faber, London, 1967
25 Kites that Fly.
Leslie L. Hunt
Dover Publications Inc., New York,
1971
Mai-Tzu and the Kite Emperor.
Wolfgang Grasse
Angus & Robertson Ltd., Sydney,
1973
Paper and Printing in Ancient China.
Berthold Laufer
Lenox Hill, New York, 1973
The Story of Gunpowder.
Kenneth Allen
Wayland Publishers Ltd., London,
1973
Hand and Brain in China.
Joseph Needham
Anglo Chinese Educational Institute,
London, 1971
Science and Civilisation in China
(vol. 1 and vol. 4 pt. 2).
Joseph Needham
Cambridge University Press,
Cambridge, 1954

Arts and Crafts

Ancient Chinese Patterns.
Published in Hong Kong
China: A Cultural Heritage.
*Marjorie Norman & Peter Evans
(compilers)*
Jackdaw Publications, London
Chinese Art and Culture.
Rene Grousset
Andre Deutsch Ltd., London, 1959
Chinese Blue and White.
Ann Frank
Studio Vista Ltd., London, 1969
Chinese Carpets and Rugs.
Adolf Hackmack
Dover Publications Inc., New York,
1973
Chinese Export Art in the 18th
Century.
Margaret Jourdain & R. Soame Jenyns
Spring Books, London, 1951
Chinese Folk Designs.
W. M. Hawley
Dover Publications Inc., New York,
1949

The Giraffe in History and Art.
Berthold Laufer
Field Museum of Natural History,
Chicago, 1928
Chinese Household Furniture.
George N. Kates
Dover Publications Inc., New York,
1948
Chinese Paper-cut Pictures.
Nancy Kuo
Alec Tiranti Ltd., London, 1964
The Chinese Puppet Theatre.
Sergei Obraztsov
(trans. J. T. MacDermott)
Faber & Faber, London, 1961
The Cooking of China.
Emily Hahn
Time-Life Books, London & New
York, 1976
Folk Arts of New China.
Foreign Languages Press
Foreign Languages Press, Peking,
1954
Taiwan Folk Art.
Shiy De-Jinn
Lion Art Book Co., Taipei
The Story of the Willow-Pattern
Plate.
Reprinted from The Family Friend
magazine 1849.
John Baker (Publishers) Ltd.,
London, 1970

Games and Puzzles

The Game of Mah Jong.
Max Robertson
Whitcoulls Ltd., Christchurch, New
Zealand, 1938
Games Ancient and Oriental and
How to Play them.
Edward Falkener
Dover Publications Inc., New York,
1961
Games of the Orient.
Stewart Culin
Reprint by Charles E. Tuttle Co.,
New York, 1967
Go and Go-Moku.
Edward Lasker
Dover Publications Inc., New York,
1934/1960
The Eighth Book of Tan.
Peter Van Note
Dover Publications Inc., New York,
1968
Tangram Teasers.
R. C. Bell
Corbitt & Hunter Ltd., Newcastle
upon Tyne, 1965

Fairy Tales and Mythology

Chinese Fairy Tales.
Leslie Bonnet
Frederick Muller Ltd., London, 1973
Chinese Folk Tales.
Richard Wilhelm (trans. E. Osers)
G. Bell & Sons Ltd., London, 1971
The Classic Fairy Tales.
Iona and Peter Opie
Oxford University Press, London,
1974
Chinese Mythology.
Anthony Christie
Hamlyn Publishing Group Ltd.,
Feltham, 1973

Chin-Pao and the Giant Pandas.
Chiang Yee
Country Life Publications, London,
1939
A Cycle of Chinese Festivities.
C. S. Wong
Malaysia Publishing House Ltd.,
Singapore, 1967
Myths of China and Japan.
D. A. Mackenzie
Gresham Publishing Co., London
The Herd Boy and the Ox and other
Chinese folk stories.
Tao Tao Sanders
Oxford University Press, London,
1971
Peiping Nursery Rhymes.
Tzu-Shih Chen (ed.)
Great China Book Co., Taipei,
Taiwan
Pidgin English Sing-Song.
Charles G. Leland
Kegan Paul Trench, London, 1897
Stories of Old China.
W. W. Yen (trans.)
Commercial Press Ltd., Hong Kong,
1962
Strange Stories from a Chinese
Studio.
H. A. Giles (trans.)
Dover Books Ltd., New York, 1961
Tales of a Chinese Grandmother.
Frances Carpenter
Charles E. Tuttle Co., Rutland, 1973

Travellers' Reports

A Journey from St Petersburg to
Pekin 1719—1722.
John Bell
Edinburgh University Press,
Edinburgh, 1965
Child Life in China.
Mary Bishop
Religious Tract Society, London,
1900
Chine.
Armand Gatti
Editions du Seuil, Paris, 1965
La Chine dans un Miroir.
Claude Roy
Editions Clairfontaine, Lausanne,
1953
The Chinese.
John Francis Davis
Penguin Books, London, 1943
Dans la Tartarie.
Rev. Peré Regis-Evariste Huc
Librairie Plon, Paris, 1925
L'Empire Chinois.
Rev. Peré Regis-Evariste Huc
Librairie de Gaume Freres, Paris,
1857
Faces of China: Tomorrow Today
Yesterday.
Photos: Pat Fok. Text: Ross Terill
Michael Joseph Ltd., London, 1974
The Middle Kingdom.
S. Wells Williams
Charles Scribner's Sons, New York,
1899
Nagel's Encyclopedia Guide to
China.
Nagel
Nagel, Geneva, 1968

The Pool of Ch'ien Lung.
Lady Hosie
Hodder & Stoughton Ltd., London,
1944
Red Star over China.
Edgar Snow
Victor Gollancz Ltd., London, 1937
Report from a Chinese Village.
Jan Myrdal
W. Heinemann Ltd., London, 1965
Social Life of the Chinese.
Rev. Justus Doolittle
Sampson Low, Son and Marston,
London, 1868
The Travels of Marco Polo.
Professor Aldo Ricci (trans.)
Routledge, Kegan and Paul, London,
1931
The Wall has Two Sides.
Felix Greene
Jonathan Cape Ltd., London, 1962

History

Chinese Looking Glass.
Dennis Bloodworth
Penguin Books Ltd., London, 1967
A Chinese View of China.
John Gittings
British Broadcasting Corporation,
London, 1973
China under the Empress Dowager.
J. O. P. Bland & E. Backhouse
W. Heinemann Ltd., London, 1910
Everyday Life in Early Imperial
China.
Michael Loewe
Faber & Faber Ltd., London, 1946
Foreign Mud.
Maurice Collis
Wayland Publishers Ltd., London,
1973
Genghis Khan and the Mongols.
Michael Gibson
Thames & Hudson Ltd., London,
1973
Half the World: The History and
Culture of China and Japan.
Arnold Toynbee (ed.)
Penguin Books Ltd., London, 1956
A History of Modern China.
Kenneth Scott Latourette
Penguin Books Ltd., London, 1956
Imperial China.
Franz Schurmann & Orville Schell (eds.)
Penguin Books Ltd., London, 1967
On the Long March.
Chen Chang-Feng
Foreign Languages Press, Peking,
1972
Shu Ching Book of History.
James Legge (trans.)
Allen & Unwin, London, 1971
Source Materials in Chinese History.
Charles Meyer & Ian Allen
Frederick Warne & Co, London,
1970

INDEX

THE SCROLL OF A HUNDRED THANKS

Had this book been printed in Chinese, these last pages would have been the first. This is therefore the appropriate place to thank all those whose gifts and talents have combined to produce it. For its faults the author is, of course, solely responsible.

Expert Advice

Dr Roderick Whitfield of the British Museum

Yu-Ling Brown of the British Library

Elizabeth Chin

Kareen King

Joanna Waley Cohen

Neil Duncan Taylor

Drawings, Maps & Charts

Chan Hung Yue

Kwok Siu Wing

Design & Layout

Melvyn Gill

Photography

Bob Croxford

Melvyn Gill

Sally and Peter Greenhill

Alastair Smith

Toys

The doll on the cover and the clockwork ping-pong match belong to Mary Hillier

The toys bought from street pedlars in Peking and the skeleton leaf painting belong to Nan Green

The French tin toy, page 172 belongs to Jean Ogilvie

All the other toys illustrated are in Pollock's Toy Museum

Picture Credits

Bob Croxford: pages 30, 38, 43, 46, 47, 58, 65, 68a, 69, 71, 73, 74, 77a, 77b, 78, 79, 82, 84, 86, 87, 94, 95, 97, 112, 123, 130, 131, 138, 143, 147, 149, 150, 151, 153, 155, 167, 172, 174b, 177, 178.

Melvyn Gill: pages 23, 26, 27, 34, 50, 51, 53, 55, 56, 57, 60, 68b, 83, 85, 92, 101, 107, 122, 134, 139, 142, 144, 148b, 157, 162, 164, 165b, 168, 169, 173, 176.

Sally & Peter Greenhill: pages 45, 54, 89, 99, 117a, 118, 136, 156.

Alastair Smith: pages 47, 154.

S.A.C.U.: page 119a.

Transworld Agency: Flashcards page 30.

Dr Roderick Whitfield: Fireworks page 31.

Institutions:

The Trustees of the British Museum for permission to reproduce the Scroll of A Hundred Sons and for the pictures on pages 108, 109, 163, 165a, 166.

Boston Museum of Fine Arts: page 45.

The Royal Pavilion Brighton: pages 63, 67.

The Cleveland Museum of Art: page 19.

The Metropolitan Museum of Art: pages 126, 127.

Publications

China Pictorial: pages 18, 20, 45, 77c, 110, 114, 115, 116b, 129, 152.

Collet's Chinese Bookshop Catalogue: pages 48, 49.

"Elle": page 120.

Publishers

For permission to quote:

Anglo Chinese Educational Institute
Hands & Brain in China
Dr Joseph Needham

Granada Publishing Co
The Crippled Tree
Han Suyin

Hodder & Stoughton
The Pool of Ch'ien Ling
Lady Hosie

Methuen & Co Ltd
A Chinese Childhood
Chiang Yee